AIRCRAFT OF THE RAF
a pictorial record 1918-1978

AIRCRAFT OF THE RAF
a pictorial record 1918-1978

compiled and edited by Paul Ellis

Macdonald and Jane's · London

Copyright © Macdonald and Jane's 1978
First published in 1978 by
Macdonald and Jane's Publishers Ltd
Paulton House, 8 Shepherdess Walk
London N1 7LW

Second impression 1979

Printed in Great Britain by
Netherwood Dalton & Co Ltd

Designed by Judy Tuke

ISBN 0 354 01183 9 (Cased)   0 354 01184 7 (Limp)

Photograph Credits

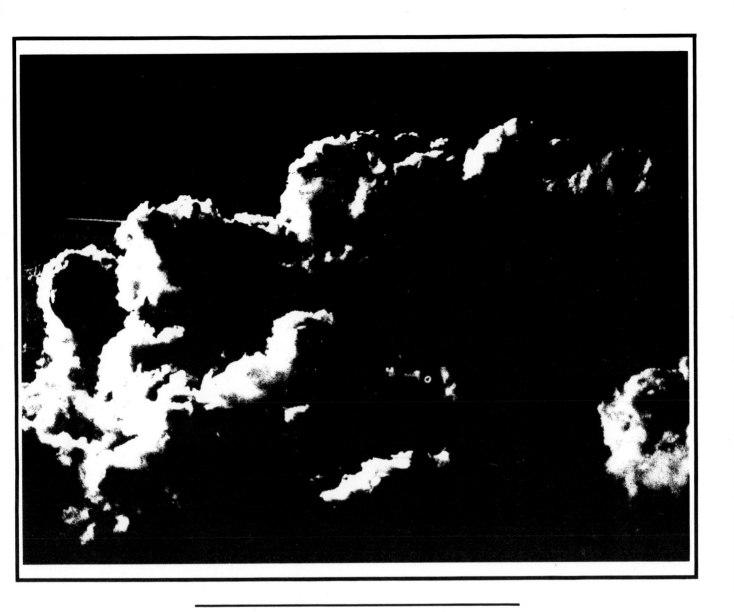

Contents

Foreword by Chief of the Air Staff

Anyone who picks up this book for other than a casual glance is likely to have more than a passing interest in flying and aeroplanes, even if it is subconscious. There is nothing unusual in that; the prospect of flight has fascinated man since earliest civilisation and, who knows, probably before. This fascination has only been translated into practical reality during the last century and the developments in aircraft technology within a single life span have been beyond man's wildest dreams.

On 1st April 1978 the Royal Air Force celebrated the 60th Anniversary of its formation. This book traces our history through the aircraft we have flown. The photographs can only give a fleeting impression into the spirit that drove the men that designed, built and flew the machines, but the imagination can more easily transport the reader into their minds, to share perhaps a faint reflection of their exhilaration and courage, their hopes and fears.

The spirit of adventure, the desire to conquer the elements in whatever form it manifests itself – is an integral part of man's inner soul. The challenge of flight, and particularly the challenge of flying and operating a high performance aircraft to the limit of its capabilities, has fired the enthusiasm of young men since the aeroplane first became a weapon of war. It is this spirit that has carried the Royal Air Force "through the Steeps to the Stars" throughout its 60 years and which I am confident will continue to do so long as men shake off the shackles of earth and fly.

Air Chief Marshal Sir Michael Beetham GCB CBE DFC AFC ADC

Introduction by J W R Taylor

There is a youthful arrogance about the name of the Royal Air Force that belies this Service's sixty years. Note that it is not the Royal British Air Force, just *the* Royal Air Force, suggesting that its deeds rather than a title distinguish it from the dozen other air forces that still retain a regal prefix in a changing world. And who would dispute this?

In November of the year in which it was born, it had 22,647 aircraft – many more than the combined first-line strengths of the present-day US and Soviet air forces. There were, of course, no supersonic warplanes, nuclear weapons or intercontinental ballistic missiles in 1918; but it is doubtful whether the survivors of the Great War, which ended in that far-off Autumn, could have imagined anything more terrible than the mud and blood of the Western Front in France.

When the war had begun, in 1914, the vague concept of air power had been symbolised by Germany's huge bomb-carrying Zeppelin airships. Aeroplanes were generally regarded as reconnaissance vehicles of dubious value; and it was not until they had demonstrated their potential as 'aerial cavalry', able to keep track of every movement of armies on the ground in daylight, that fighter aircraft had to be pressed into service to restrict their activities. Bombers also started their career by attacking the bases of 'the other side's' airships and reconnaissance aircraft.

The use of aeroplanes for strategic bombing of targets in the enemy homeland, rather than in the immediate battle area, was pioneered by the French and Italian air forces, and the Royal Naval Air Service, in 1914-15. By 1917, the Germans were setting the pace, by sending formations of twin-engined Gothas over London in daylight. This led to such a public outcry against the ineffectiveness of Britain's air defences, and the whole system of acquiring and operating its military aircraft, that an Air Ministry was created to take control of these aspects of the nation's war effort, and the original Royal Flying Corps and Royal Naval Air Service were combined to form the Royal Air Force on April 1st, 1918.

First Chief of the Air Staff was Major-General Sir Hugh (later Viscount) Trenchard, who had earlier commanded the RFC on active service. He soon found it less easy to work with the Secretary of State than it had been to steer the RFC through the period of the 'Fokker Scourge', when Germany's Fokker monoplanes, armed with a synchronised forward-firing machine-gun, had almost succeeded in shooting the Allied air forces from the sky. Britain's aircraft designers had then ended the Fokker's reign by producing a succession of fighters that began with the D.H.2 and F.E.2b and culminated in the Camel, most successful fighter of the war, and S.E.5. But it was their simultaneous evolution of big bombers that held a particular fascination for Trenchard.

Asked to build 'a bloody paralyser of an aeroplane', Frederick Handley Page had produced the twin-engined O/100 and O/400 night bombers, each able to carry sixteen 112 lb bombs or a single 1,650-pounder. Trenchard resigned as CAS and took up an appointment instead as commander of the new Independent Force, formed for the sole purpose of maintaining an all-out offensive against German munitions factories. Never before had an air force been freed of the shackles of responsibility for, or control by, troops on the ground. The success of the experiment shaped the whole future pattern of British air power.

Heart of the Independent Force was its four squadrons of O/100s and O/400s, supported by six squadrons of F.E.2b night bombers, D.H.4, D.H.9 and D.H.9a day bombers, and Sopwith Camel escort fighters. During the last five months of the war, they dropped 390 tons of bombs by night and 160 tons by day. Two-fifths of the total fell on enemy airfields with the result that raids on Allied airfields almost ceased and not a single aeroplane was destroyed by German bombing throughout the lifetime of Independent Force. The remaining 330 tons of bombs were aimed at poison gas plants, aircraft and aero-engine factories, railways, and buildings housing blast furnaces. The targets were photographed subsequently by high-flying reconnaissance aircraft, to discover whether or not further raids were required.

Had the war not ended on November 11th, 1918, the weight of attack would have increased enormously. The first squadron of Handley Page V/1500 four-engined bombers, each able to carry up to thirty 250-lb bombs, were poised on the RAF airfield at Bircham Newton, in Norfolk, from where they could have flown all the way to Berlin and back.

Trenchard never forgot the lessons he had learned with Independent Force. Back in command, as the postwar Chief of Air Staff, he compiled a document known officially as *Cmd. 467. Permanent Organisation of the Royal Air Force,* for presentation to the House of Commons by the new Secretary of State for Air, Winston Churchill. Army and Navy leaders were horrified by the suggestion that the upstart war baby could even be considered as a permanent third Service. The contents of what is remembered today as 'Trenchard's White Paper' could well have given them apoplexy.

Cmd. 467 cost one 1919 penny from His Majesty's Stationery Office, for which the public could purchase the most remarkable blueprint for national survival in the history of aerial warfare. Its basic theme was expounded in a single paragraph:

"In planning the formation of the peacetime Royal Air Force it has been assumed that no need will arise for some years at least for anything in the nature of general mobilisation. It has been possible therefore to concentrate attention on providing for the needs of the moment as far as they can be foreseen and on laying the foundations of a highly-trained and efficient force which, though not capable of expansion in its present form, can be made so without any drastic alteration should necessity arise in years to come. Broadly speaking, the principle has been to reduce service squadrons to the minimum considered essential for our garrisons overseas with a very small number in the United Kingdom as a reserve, and to concentrate the whole of the remainder of our resources on perfecting the training of officers and men."

The architect of the plan summed it up less formally in one sentence: "I have laid the foundations for a castle; if nobody builds anything bigger than a cottage on them, it will at least be a very good cottage."

It proved to be just that. What had been a mighty wartime armada of 291,170 officers and men, in 188 combat squadrons and 15 flights, was shrunk rapidly to a mere 33 squadrons. For a period, a single flight of Vimy biplanes represented the RAF's entire home-based heavy bomber force. As late as 1935, when King George V reviewed the Royal Air Force on his Silver Jubilee, the formidable new monoplane bombers of Hitler's reborn Luftwaffe were matched in Britain by Virginias, big fabric-covered

biplanes that lumbered along at less than 100 mph (160 km/h).

Only in retrospect is it possible to appreciate how sturdy and professional were the foundations under the 'tween-wars fabric tepee.

In 1922, Churchill had presented the RAF with an unprecedented challenge, by making it entirely responsible for keeping the peace in what is now Iraq. Throughout history, warlike tribes in the Middle East had fought fiercely among each other and against any intruders into their territory. To keep them in check by traditional methods, under postwar mandates, was proving far too costly. So, the troops were removed, and their place was taken by two squadrons of RAF Vernon transports, supported by six squadrons of wartime-vintage D.H.9as, Bristol Fighters and Snipes, a mixed Brigade of British and Indian infantry, some native levies, and four squadrons of armoured cars. Thus was launched the policy of air control, extended subsequently throughout the Middle East and as far as Egypt, Somaliland and the Northwest Frontier of India.

Well-meaning people have often suggested that air control was inhumane. In fact, it saved countless lives. If a tribe became rebellious, or began raiding its neighbours, a message was dropped from an aircraft, threatening an air attack on its village if the men did not put away their guns. If they refused to do so, and the attack had to be made, it was usual to warn the inhabitants well in advance, so that they lost their possessions but not their lives.

One operation of this kind, against the Mahsud tribes in Waziristan, checked their outrages within two months at the cost of two lives. A campaign on the ground against the same tribesmen, in 1919, had caused 1,329 casualties and achieved nothing.

The first-ever airlift of troops took place in February 1923, when a large force of Kurds and hill Arabs decided to seize Kirkuk in Iraq. As the only possible way of saving the town, 480 officers and men of the 14th Sikhs were flown to Kirkuk in the air control Vernons. The sight of them was enough to make the invaders give up terrorising the people of the town and melt away like magic into the hills.

Air control demanded a blend of patience, skill and courage that bred superb aircrew, and great leaders. They began to receive the fine aircraft they deserved as warclouds began to gather over Europe in the late thirties.

It is fashionable today to belittle what Britain achieved in the second World War. The fighter pilots who won the Battle of Britain have been portrayed as inferior to the enemy they defeated. The

RAF bombing which did much to take the heart out of the German people, as well as helping to burn more than 500 acres out of the heart of each of 31 German cities, is dismissed as a cruel waste of effort. Trenchard becomes a bigoted backer of all the wrong horses, Churchill a warmonger who made endless mistakes and misjudgements.

The critics should, rather, thank God for the fact that they are free to criticise, and live in a land which faced the apparently invincible Nazi war machine without powerful allies at one of history's darkest hours. Those who lived in Britain in October 1940 – and perhaps even in New York and Moscow – did not doubt from whence their salvation had come.

For the first half of its sixty years, the RAF was never at peace. Always there was a war somewhere in the world in which its men had to live with the daily risk of death – or worse at the hands of primitive tribesmen. Since 1948, it has been called upon to play its part in the near-bloodless victory of the Berlin Airlift, in campaigns in Malaya and Cyprus, against the Mau Mau in Kenya, in Aden and Korea, and at Suez. It has stood guard constantly on the NATO side of the iron curtain that divides former allies in Europe, inside Quick Reaction Alert hangars from which its fighters still scramble to investigate aircraft that probe Britain's defences ceaselessly, and on the frontiers of peoples under its protection as far away as Belize in Central America.

In its time, the RAF has held many world speed and distance records, and won for Britain the coveted Schneider Trophy. It continues to rescue people of many nations from perils of sea, flood and snow; to drop food to the starving; find those who are lost; and lift gently to hospital those who might otherwise die. It pioneered concepts of flying training that are now standard throughout the world, and is still demonstrating entirely novel combat techniques with its unique V/STOL Harrier.

It no longer has a force of long-range strategic bombers of the kind that Trenchard considered so essential; but its responsibilities too have changed, and it is now part of a multi-national organisation that can command combat aircraft of every conceivable kind. The aircraft it does have are as good as any in the world; its men have never been better trained.

The RAF motto is *Per Ardua ad Astra,* meaning "Through Difficulties to the Stars". For sixty years, the Service has had to face a multiplicity of difficulties. Some of the stars are in this book.

JWRT

1918-1928

R.E.8

The R.E.8 was designed by the Royal Aircraft Factory at Farnborough as a two-seat corps-reconnaissance aircraft and first flew in mid-1916. Known colloquially as the 'Harry Tate', the R.E.8 entered service in November 1916 after certain modifications had been made to reduce its proneness to spinning. Powered by a 150-hp RAF .4A engine, it had a maximum speed of 102 mph and was armed with a .303-in Lewis gun on a Scarff ring-mounting in the rear cockpit. At the time of the Armistice in November 1918, the RAF had 1,913 R.E.8s on strength, equipping nineteen squadrons. Postwar it served with Nos 6, 30, and 208 Squadrons, all abroad.

R.E.8 serial number A 4173 was one of a batch built by the Daimler Co. Ltd., in Coventry, while the line-up of R.E.8s was photographed in Egypt during the First World War.

B.E.2e

The two-seat B.E.2e, which entered service with No 21 Squadron RFC in July 1916, was another Royal Aircraft Factory design used for corps-reconnaissance. Slow and rather too stable for rapid manoeuvrability, the B.E.2e, and indeed its predecessor the B.E.2c, nevertheless remained in RAF service after the Armistice, equipping Nos 30, 31, 114 and 269 Squadrons. A few were also used by training schools. Powered by a 90-hp RAF. 1A engine, top speed was a gentlemanly 82 mph.

de Havilland D.H.4

The de Havilland (Airco) D.H.4 was first delivered to No 55 Squadron RFC in March 1917 for use as a light day-bomber, carrying up to 460 lb of bombs on racks beneath the fuselage and wings. It was armed with a fixed .303-in Vickers gun, with Constantinesco synchronising gear, mounted on the left side of the fuselage, and one or two Lewis guns on the rear Scarff ring-mounting. By the end of the war this Eagle-engined aircraft was still in service with Nos 18, 25, 55, 57, 202, 217 and 244 Squadrons.

A total of 1,449 was built in Britain; American production of the Liberty-engined variant ran to more than 4,500. The D.H.4 shown here is fitted with the 200-hp RAF.3A engine.

S.E.5A

Generally accepted as being the best military aircraft to be produced by the Royal Aircraft Factory at Farnborough, and one of the best of the First World War, the S.E.5A was developed from the S.E. (Scout Experimental) 5, which first entered service with No 56 Squadron in March 1917. Powered by either a 200, 220 or 240-hp Hispano-Suiza or 200-hp Wolseley Viper engine, the S.E.5A was capable of a maximum speed of 132 mph. Armament varied slightly from squadron to squadron but typically consisted of one .303-in Vickers with Constantinesco synchronising gear mounted on the left of the fuselage, and one .303-in Lewis gun on a Foster mount on the upper wing. Provision was also made for a four 25-lb bomb carrier under the wings. At the end of the war the RAF had 2,696 S.E.5s and S.F.5As equipping Nos 1, 24, 29, 32, 40, 41, 50, 56, 60, 64, 68, 74, 84, 85, 92, 94, 111, 145, 150 and 229 Squadrons.

The S.E.5A shown here is fitted with an experimental 200-hp Wolseley Viper with underslung radiator and was photographed in February or March 1918. The production-line shown below is of standard aircraft at the Austin Motor Co. Ltd., Birmingham, also in 1918.

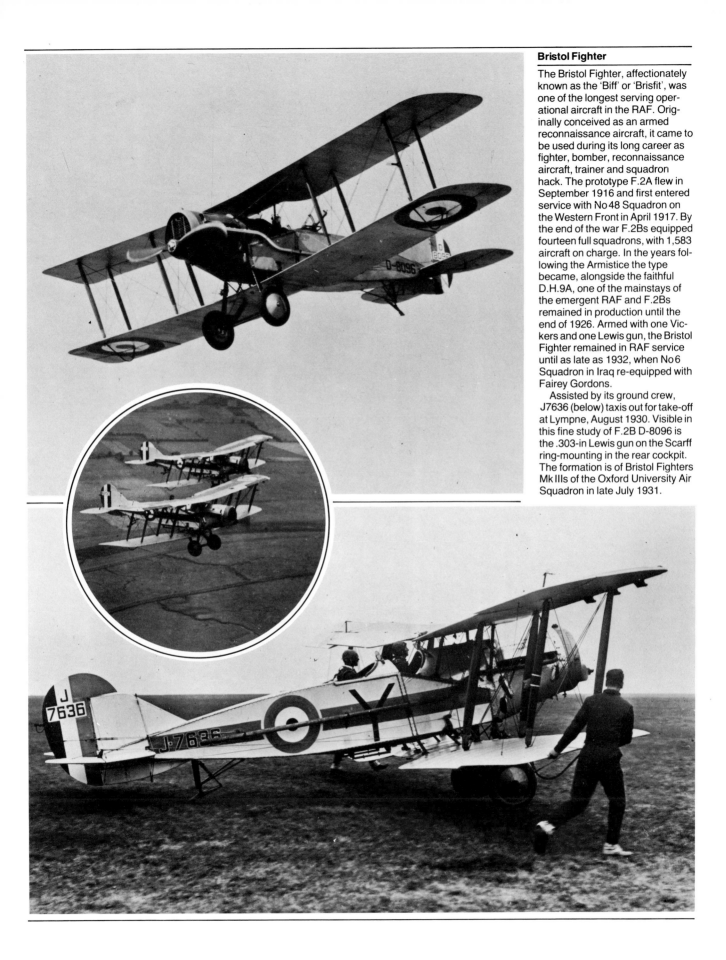

Bristol Fighter

The Bristol Fighter, affectionately known as the 'Biff' or 'Brisfit', was one of the longest serving operational aircraft in the RAF. Originally conceived as an armed reconnaissance aircraft, it came to be used during its long career as fighter, bomber, reconnaissance aircraft, trainer and squadron hack. The prototype F.2A flew in September 1916 and first entered service with No 48 Squadron on the Western Front in April 1917. By the end of the war F.2Bs equipped fourteen full squadrons, with 1,583 aircraft on charge. In the years following the Armistice the type became, alongside the faithful D.H.9A, one of the mainstays of the emergent RAF and F.2Bs remained in production until the end of 1926. Armed with one Vickers and one Lewis gun, the Bristol Fighter remained in RAF service until as late as 1932, when No 6 Squadron in Iraq re-equipped with Fairey Gordons.

Assisted by its ground crew, J7636 (below) taxis out for take-off at Lympne, August 1930. Visible in this fine study of F.2B D-8096 is the .303-in Lewis gun on the Scarff ring-mounting in the rear cockpit. The formation is of Bristol Fighters Mk IIIs of the Oxford University Air Squadron in late July 1931.

Sopwith Camel

Probably the most famous British fighter of the First World War, the Sopwith Camel first went into action on the Western Front in July 1917 with No 70 Squadron, RFC. Powered by a 110-hp Le Rhône or 130-hp Clerget rotary engine the Camel was capable of a top speed of about 113 mph. It was normally armed with a pair of .303-in Vickers machine guns synchronised to fire through the propeller arc and was unquestionably an outstanding fighting machine, although unforgiving towards inexperienced or careless pilots. At the time of the Armistice the RAF had more than 2,600 of the type on charge, equipping some thirty-two squadrons.

Shown here is a Camel F.1 at an RFC training unit during the First World War, and below, Camel B 2312 was one of a batch built by Ruston, Proctor & Co. Ltd.

Armstrong Whitworth F.K.8

The Armstrong Whitworth F.K.8 two-seat reconnaissance bomber equipped five RAF squadrons at home and three overseas at the end of the First World War. Powered by a 160-hp Beardmore engine this functional looking aeroplane could manage a top speed of 95 mph. Armament was a forward-firing synchronised .303-in Vickers and a .303-in Lewis gun on a Scarff ring-mounting administered by the observer. Bomb load was 160 lb and endurance around three hours.

Noticeable in this photograph, of September 1918 vintage, is the huge manufacturer's plaque on the nose of the 'Big Ack'.

Sopwith Dolphin

Less attractive than the earlier Pup and Camel, the single-seat Sopwith Dolphin with its back-staggered wings was nevertheless a formidable machine in the right hands, particularly those of Nos 19 and 79 Squadron pilots. It first entered service with No 19 squadron RFC in January 1918 and by the end of the war equipped a total of five RAF squadrons. It was powered by the bulky 200-hp Hispano-Suiza engine giving it a maximum speed of around 125 mph. Armament was a hefty two .303-in Vickers guns synchronised to fire through the propeller arc, and one or two .303-in Lewis guns firing obliquely upwards through the wing centre section. The two Lewis guns are clearly visible in this photograph of Dolphin C3786, one of a batch of 500 aircraft ordered from Sopwith.

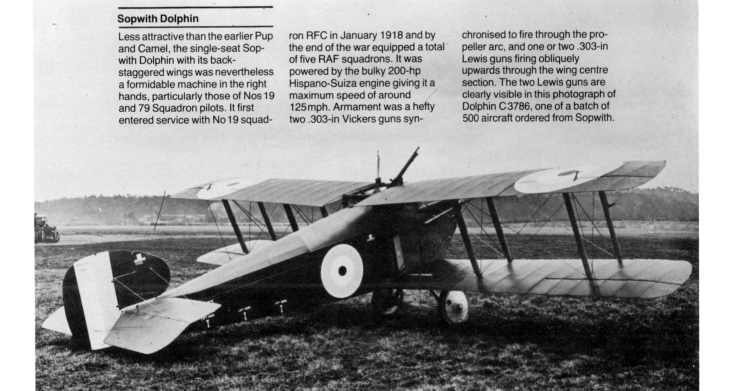

Avro 504K

A.V. Roe built his first 504 in 1913, and during the early part of the First World War the type was in front-line service with both the RFC and RNAS for bombing and reconnaissance. The 504K first appeared in 1918 and differed from its predecessor, the 504J, in having a modified cowling and engine bearers to take a variety of rotary engines, including the 110-hp Le Rhône, 130-hp Clerget or 100-hp Monoscupape. At the time of the Armistice, the RAF possessed about 3,000 out of a total of more than 8,300 Avro 504s of all Marks built during the War. After the war the the 504K equipped the Central Flying School and Nos 1, 2, 3, 4 and 5 Flying Training Schools and remained in service until replaced by the 504N in the mid-1920s. Maximum speed was 95 mph at sea level and 85 mph at 10,000 ft, the aircraft taking sixteen minutes to reach that altitude.

Caught half-way round a loop, E 4222 carries its manufacturer's name proudly, and prominently, on the side of the fuselage. The photograph was taken at Hounslow in May 1919. Below: E 4342 is of similar vintage and was built by the Eastbourne Aviation Co. Ltd.

de Havilland D.H.9A

Classified as a two-seat day bomber, the D.H.9A first entered service with No 110 Squadron in June 1918 and continued in RAF service until as late as 1931. Built by Westland at Yeovil the 'Nine-ack' managed a maximum speed of 114 mph on its 400-hp Liberty engine. Armament was a fixed forward-firing .303-in Vickers and a Lewis gun aft; bomb load was a respectable 450 lb and No 110 Squadron's D.H.9As had dropped more than ten tons of bombs on Germany by the Armistice. The 9A was standard equipment with UK-based bomber squadrons until replaced by the Fairey Fawn in the mid-1920s; it also served widely with the Auxiliary Air Force and with training schools.

This Airco-built aircraft started life as a D.H.9 but was subsequently modified by the Westland Aircraft Works to become one of the prototype D.H.9As. Engine was the 350-hp Rolls-Royce Eagle. Above: D.H.9As of No 39 Squadron rehearsing for Hendon, June 1926.

Handley Page O /400

The Handley Page O/400 was the RAF's standard heavy bomber during the First World War and was an improved version of Frederick Handley Page's O/100, built to satisfy Commander Murray Sueter's request for a 'bloody paralyser of an aircraft'. At the end of the war it equipped Nos 58, 97, 100, 115, 207, 214, 215 and 216 Squadrons of the RAF and soldiered on for a while before being replaced by the Vimy and D.H. 10 Amiens. Two squadrons, Nos 70 and 216, were operating O/400s in Egypt until 1920. Powered by a pair of Rolls-Royce Eagles it could manage a top speed of 97 mph and carried a maximum bomb load of eight 250-lb bombs or sixteen 112-lb bombs internally.

Flying the O/400 was a windy business, the pilot being protected only by a small semi-circular windscreen.

Sopwith Snipe

Introduced as a successor to the ubiquitous Camel, the single-seat two-bay Sopwith Snipe reached the RAF in France only a few weeks before the end of the First World War; nevertheless it was given the opportunity to prove the soundness of its design as a warplane and was found to be fast, manoeuvrable and strong. Powered by the 230-hp Bentley B.R.2 nine-cylinder rotary engine, the Snipe was capable of a top speed of 121 mph and was armed with twin .303-in Vickers guns synchronised to fire through the propeller arc. Snipes were also equipped to carry four 20-lb bombs or even a single 112-lb bomb. At home, Snipes remained in service with No 43 Squadron based at RAF Henlow until replaced by Gloster Gamecocks in August 1926. Altogether the type served with thirteen home-based and four overseas squadrons after the war and was a regular performer at the famous Hendon displays during the 1920s.

Left; one of the prototype Snipes, photographed in March 1918. Although of poor quality this formation photograph (below) of No 1 Squadron Snipes near Baghdad is nevertheless of interest for its rarity value.

Short 320

The Short 320 seaplane was the last of many types of Short seaplane to enter service during the First World War and was used for anti-submarine patrol and naval reconnaissance. Preceded by the Short 184, the type served with Nos 266 and 268 Squadrons. More than 300 Short 184s and fifty Short 320s were in RAF service at the war's end.

Receiving the attentions of the crane crew is a torpedo-armed Short 184 prototype.

Felixstowe F.5

Too late to see action in the First World War, the Felixstowe F.5 became the standard flying boat in RAF service in the subsequent years and equipped nine squadrons at home and overseas. Powered by a pair of Rolls-Royce Eagle VIII engines, top speed was a sedate 88 mph and duration was 7 hours. The Felixstowe F.5 remained in service with No 230 Squadron (re-numbered No 480 Flight at the end of 1922) on naval co-operation tasks until superseded by Southamptons in 1925. Armament for the anti-submarine role was four 230-lb bombs, with single Lewis guns mounted in the bow, dorsal and beam positions.

N4043 and N4193 are seen here at Calshot, date unknown.

Handley Page V /1500

The four-engined Handley Page V/1500 has an important place in RAF history as the Service's first true strategic bomber, being designed to strike at strategic targets in the heart of Germany from bases in the UK. It was not destined to see active service in Europe, however, and was operational with the RAF, with Nos 166 and 167 Squadrons, for only a short time after the war before being superseded by the smaller twin-engined Vickers Vimy. Powered by four Rolls-Royce Eagle VIII engines (or Galloway Atlantic or Napier Lion engines) mounted back-to-back, it could lift a bomb load of two 3,300-lb or thirty 250-lb bombs and had a range of 1,300 miles at a cruising speed of 80 mph. 'If this aeroplane did not bomb Berlin,' said Frederick Handley Page in 1919, 'we may find consolation in the fact that perhaps the Germans knew it was coming and saw it was time to give up.'

de Havilland D.H.10 Amiens

The original D.H.10, which first flew in March 1918, had its twin engines mounted as pushers like those of the earlier D.H.3; the second prototype, which flew a month later, adopted the more conventional tractor layout for its Rolls-Royce Eagle VIIIs. Found to be faster than the D.H.9 and capable of carrying twice the bomb load, the type was quickly put into production with some 1,291 being ordered. Only a few reached squadrons of the Independent Force before the Armistice and contracts were drastically cut back or cancelled; nevertheless about 220 were completed and served with No 120 Squadron at home and Nos 60 (later re-numbered 97) and 216 Squadrons overseas after the war. More than half of the final production run was of the improved Amiens IIIA, with 400-hp Liberty engines mounted on the lower wings. These were capable of a maximum speed of 126 mph.

These two photographs show clearly the difference between the earlier Eagle-engined Amiens II (right) and the improved Liberty-engined Mk IIIA (below).

Vickers Vimy

The Vickers Vimy was the third of the new generation of heavy bombers designed to attack Berlin with the Independent Force; but unlike the D.H.10 and V/1500 the Vimy was to enjoy a particularly long career with the RAF, serving not only as a bomber but also in later years as a parachute trainer at Henlow. The first Vimys reached the RAF too late to participate in the First World War, equipping No 58 Squadron in Egypt in July 1919 and at home D Flight of No 100 Squadron at Spittlegate. The Vimy was replaced in front-line service in 1924 and 1925 by the Vickers Virginia but remained operational with No 502 Squadron in Northern Ireland until early in 1929.

Powered by two Rolls-Royce Eagle VIIIs, the Vimy had a maximum speed of 100 mph and could carry 2,476 lb of bombs. From 1926 the surviving Vimys swapped their Rolls-Royce Eagles for the more reliable and efficient Armstrong Siddeley Jaguar or Bristol Jupiter VIII radial engines.

Disgorging parachutists, three Vimys perform at the Hendon Air Display in 1929. The ground shot shows a Vimy of No 216 Squadron about to leave Heliopolis, Egypt, for Baghdad. During the early 1920s No 216 Squadron shared with Nos 45 and 70 Squadrons the task of operating the pioneer Cairo to Baghdad mail service.

Vickers Vernon

The Vickers Vernon, which first entered service with No 45 Squadron at Hinaidi, Iraq, in 1922, was the first RAF aircraft designed specifically for troop carrying duties and could carry twelve passengers at a maximum speed of 118 mph. The original aircraft were fitted with the ubiquitous Rolls-Royce Eagle VIIIs mounted midway between the wings, but it was found that these engines lacked the necessary power to give anything like the required performance in the thin, hot air of Iraq, and later aircraft were re-engined with 450-hp Napier Lion IIs. The final version of the Vernon had Napier Lion IIIs, long-range fuel tanks and had their nose-wheel removed. The all-wood Vernons were finally replaced by the larger wood-and-metal Victorias in 1927.

About sixty Vernons were built for the RAF, serving only with Nos 45 and 70 Squadrons, and although designated as troop carriers they were nonetheless not unsuccessful as bombers. This one was caught at Hendon during the Aerial Pageant of 1923.

Gloster Grebe

The Gloster Grebe was one of the fighters selected to re-equip the new peacetime RAF, first deliveries being to one flight of No 111 Squadron at Duxford in October 1923. Superseding the wartime Sopwith Snipe, the significantly faster Grebe could manage a maximum speed of 152 mph on its 400-hp Armstrong Siddeley Jaguar IV engine. A total of 129 was built for the RAF, including a number of dual control trainers, and the last Grebes in front-line service were finally superseded by Siskins in July 1929. The type equipped Nos 19, 25, 29, 32 and 56 Squadrons as well as the original flight from No 111 Squadron.

This pair of Grebes from No 25 Squadron, based at Hawkinge, was photographed taking off from Lympne in November 1927.

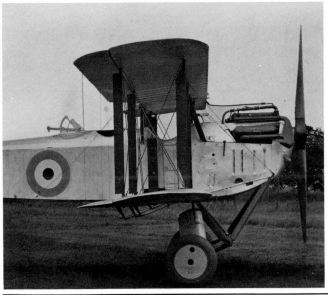

Fairey IIID

Classified by the RAF as a General Purpose aircraft, the three-seat Fairey IIID could be used as a bomber, carrying typically two 230-lb bombs, or as a spotter-reconnaissance type fitted with either wheels or floats. The majority of the IIIDs served with the Fleet Air Arm as twin-float sea-planes, the first units to be equipped receiving their aircraft in 1924. It was in its landplane form, however, that the IIID is best remembered in RAF service, specifically for its remarkable long-distance flight from England to South Africa during the latter part of 1925 and early 1926.

Avro Aldershot

Although powered only by a single 650-hp Rolls-Royce Condor III, the massive Avro Aldershot carried a bomb load of up to 2,000 lb in addition to its crew of three, a load comparable with that of some of its twin-engined contemporaries. It first entered service with No 99 Squadron at Bircham Newton in April 1924 and flew intensively with that squadron until replaced by Hyderabads in 1926. Although it is often quoted as being armed with only a single aft-firing Lewis gun, a contemporary maker's drawing shows it fitted additionally with a fixed Vickers gun for the pilot and a downward-firing ventral Lewis gun.

Fairey Fawn

The Fairey Fawn was a two-seat day bomber and was the first of its type to enter service with the RAF. Originally conceived as an Army co-operation aircraft, the Fawn first entered service with Nos 11, 12 and 100 Squadrons in 1925, replacing the D.H.9A. One of the least attractive of Fairey's otherwise functional aeroplanes, the Fawn was powered by a 470-hp Napier Lion II engine which endowed it with a top speed of 114 mph. Armament was a .303-in Vickers forward and a Lewis gun aft; bomb load was a maximum of 460 lb although aircraft of No 12 Squadron were reported to have carried bombs exceeding 500 lb in weight.

This Fawn III, J7768, was one which was fitted with a supercharged Napier Lion VI but never entered squadron service.

Armstrong Whitworth Siskin III

Entering RAF service with No 41 Squadron in May 1924, the single-seat Armstrong Whitworth Siskin III served with only two squadrons, the second being No 111 Squadron based at Duxford, and was superseded by the superior all-metal Siskin IIIA in March 1927. The IIIA was powered by the supercharged Armstrong Siddeley Jaguar IVS and had a top speed of 156 mph at sea level. About 400 were built for the RAF, including some 47 dual control trainers, by Blackburn, Bristol, Gloster, Vickers and the parent company, Armstrong Whitworth. No fewer than eleven squadrons eventually operated Siskin IIIAs, with those of No 56 Squadron remaining in service until 1932.

Perhaps the most memorable public appearance of the Siskin was at the 1930 Hendon Display when No 43 Squadron's aircraft performed tied together in squadron formation. J7148 was an original Siskin III, and J7000 was completed as the Siskin dual-control trainer prototype.

Vickers Virginia

The Vickers Virginia heavy night bomber first entered service with the RAF at the end of 1924, replacing the Vimys of Nos 7 and 58 Squadrons, and early in 1925 equipping No 9 Squadron. The type ran through ten Marks during its long service career, the most numerous of which was the Mark X, accounting for fifty out of a total production of 124. The Virginia Mark X was fitted with two 570-hp Napier Lion V engines which gave it a top speed of 108 mph, and the characteristic unsynchronised drone which accompanied the passage of this lumbering beast became a familiar night-time sound for more than a decade.

While not a very fast aeroplane, the Virginia could carry a maximum of 3,000 lb of bombs and, equipping Nos 7, 9, 10, 51, 58, 214, 215, 500 and 502 (Bomber) Squadrons, remained in front-line service until 1937. The type was also used for parachute training at the Home Aircraft Depot at Henlow and some Virginias were still flying as late as 1941.

Rigger's nightmare: a Virginia VII, showing clearly the two Napier Lion V engines. The bombed-up Virginia from No 58 Squadron is about to take off from Worth Down on a night raid, April 1932.

Hawker Woodcock

The Woodcock was the first single-seat fighter to bear the famous Hawker name and entered service with No 3 Squadron at Upavon in May 1925 as a replacement for the squadron's seven-year-old Sopwith Snipes. The only other Woodcock squadron was No 17, based at Hawkinge, Kent, which received its new aircraft in March 1926. Although initially suffering a number of accidents as a result of structural failures of one kind or another, the Woodcock ultimately became well liked as a night fighter and remained in RAF service until replaced by Gamecocks in 1928. A total of sixty-one was delivered and a few were still flying in 1936. Powered by a 420-hp Bristol Jupiter IV, the twin Vickers-armed Woodcock had a top speed of 143mph.

This flight of Woodcock IIs of No 17 Squadron was photographed at Bristol on June 30th, 1927.

Supermarine Southampton

The Supermarine Southampton was designed by R.J. Mitchell and first entered service with No 480 Coastal Reconnaissance Flight at Calshot in August 1925 as a replacement for the Felixstowe F.5. The Southampton was a military development of the civil Supermarine Swan and, powered by two 502-hp Napier Lion Vs, had a maximum range of 930 miles at a cruising speed of 83 mph. From the outset the Southampton showed its propensity for long-distance flights, and during more than a decade of front-line service the type made many record-breaking long-distance flights, perhaps the most important of which was the 27,000 mile cruise by four Mark IIs of the Far East Flight, led by Group Captain H.M. Cave-Brown-Cave, which left Felixstowe on October 14th, 1927, flying to Singapore, then to Australia and returning to Singapore in December 1928. At home, Southamptons served with Nos 201, 203, 204 and 210 Squadrons on general reconnaissance duties, and overseas with Nos 203 (Iraq) and 205 (Singapore) Squadrons. The last Southamptons were retired in September 1937.

Shown here are Southampton I and IIs from No 201 Squadron.

Handley Page Hyderabad

A heavy night bomber carrying a crew of four, the Handley Page Hyderabad was a military development of the pioneering Handley Page W.8 commercial airliner. The prototype first flew in October 1923 and appeared at the RAF Display at Hendon the following year. The last RAF heavy bomber in squadron service to be of wooden construction, the Hyderabad first entered service with No 99 Squadron at Bircham Wood in December 1925, replacing the huge single-engined Avro Aldershots. Re-equipment of the RAF in the 1920s was a leisurely affair and the second Hyderabad squadron, No 10 at Upper Heyford, was not formed until January 1928. In 1929 Hyderabads were chosen to equip Nos 502 and 503 Squadrons of the Auxiliary Air Force.

Powered by a pair of 454-hp Napier Lion engines the Hyderabad had a top speed of 109 mph at sea level and could carry 1,100 lb of bombs. A total of thirty-eight was built for the RAF and although withdrawn from front-line service by the end of 1930 it was not declared obsolete until August 1934.

Gloster Gamecock

Last of the RAF's wooden biplane fighters, the chunky Gloster Gamecock was a development of H.P. Folland's single-seat Grebe, differing primarily in having a Bristol Jupiter engine, re-positioned armament and a different tail unit. Production Gamecock Is were fitted with the 425-hp Bristol Jupiter IV, which gave the type a top speed of 155 mph at 5,000 feet, and the aircraft first equipped No 43 Squadron at Henlow in March 1926, followed in April by No 23 Squadron, which retained its aircraft until July 1931. It was at the 1931 Hendon Air Pageant that two 23 Squadron Gamecocks, flown by Flight Lieutenant M.M. Day and Pilot Officer Douglas Bader, gave a memorable display of aerobatics.

The Gamecock suffered from a certain amount of wing flutter and late in 1927 additional Vee struts were placed between the wing extensions and the interplane struts. Pilots were warned not to enter intentional right-hand spins although several pilots survived twenty-two turn left-hand spins and Gloster Chief Test Pilot Howard Saint performed a 275-mph terminal velocity dive without the aircraft disintegrating.

Vickers Victoria

Introduced as a replacement for the Vernon troop carrier, the Vickers Victoria was based on the major components of the Virginia bomber, the most noticeable difference being the substantially deeper fuselage of the transport aircraft. The first production aircraft, designated the Victoria III, flew in January 1926 and the type was accepted for service with No 70 Squadron in Iraq and No 216 Squadron in Egypt in August 1926, replacing Vernons and Vimys. As a comparison with today's prices, each of the forty-six Mark IIIs delivered cost only £9,000. The metal Victoria V was the main production type, the first of which was delivered in September 1929.

Powered by a pair of 570-hp Napier Lion XI engines the Victoria V had a top speed of 110 mph at sea level and could carry twenty-two troops in addition to its crew of two. The majority of the Victorias delivered operated overseas but one aircraft was operated by the Central Flying School for training pilots in blind flying techniques from March 1932. The last Victorias were replaced by Valentias in 1935. This photograph shows the first production Victoria VI, K3159, later to be converted to Valentia configuration.

Fairey Fox

The Fairey Fox two-seat day bomber started life as a private venture and first flew in January 1925. Its performance margin over contemporary aircraft, fighters as well as bombers, was so demonstrably great that the Chief of Air Staff of the time, Air Chief Marshal Sir Hugh Trenchard, ordered a complete squadron after seeing the prototype flying in October 1925. This squadron, No 12, based at Andover, received its aircraft in August 1926 and retained them until 1931. Only twenty-eight were built but No 12 Squadron put them to excellent use, consistently beating the fighter defences during Air Exercises and giving spectacular displays at three successive Hendon Air Pageants. Replacement of some of the American 480-hp Curtiss D-12 engines with Rolls-Royce Kestrels was carried out in the early part of 1929, the modified aircraft being designated Fox IAs. Maximum speed of the original Curtiss-engined aircraft was 156 mph at sea level, and range was 500 miles at 130 mph. The Kestrel-engined Foxes were capable of a top speed of 160 mph at sea level.

Hawker Horsley

Used by the RAF both as a two-seat day bomber and torpedo bomber, the Hawker Horsley replaced the Fairey Fawns in Nos 11 and 100 Squadrons in its bomber form in 1927, the first torpedo versions going to No 36 Squadron at Donibristle in June 1928. In all, seven squadrons operated the type and a total of 112 Horsleys was built for the RAF. The Horsleys were seen as a considerable advance over their predecessors, capable of carrying three times the bomb load over greater distances. Powered by a 665-hp Rolls-Royce Condor IIIA the bomber could muster a maximum speed of 126 mph and was armed with a fixed forward-firing Vickers and a Lewis gun aft in addition to its offensive load of 1,500 lbs of bombs or a single torpedo.

In 1929 the first all-metal aircraft started to come off the assembly line and re-equipped No 36 Squadron bound for service in Singapore. All Horsleys had been replaced in the UK by February 1934, although No 36 Squadron's aircraft in Singapore were not replaced until 1935.

Shown here are J7721, second Horsley prototype, photographed in 1926, and J8006 with torpedo slung beneath the fuselage, photographed in January 1927.

Avro 504N

Popularly known as the Lynx-Avro, the 504N was designed as a replacement for the wartime Avro 504K. The first production model flew in 1927 and the type remained in production until 1933; a total of 570 was built, including seventy-eight conversions from old 504Ks. The type was used as a standard trainer by No 1 Flying Training School at Netheravon, No 2 FTS at Digby, No 3 FTS at Grantham, No 4 FTS in Egypt and No 5 FTS at Sealand as well as being gainfully employed as a communications aircraft by No 24 Squadron at Kenley and by numerous Auxiliary Air Force squadrons.

Lynx-Avros of the Central Flying School at Wittering were the first aircraft to teach blind flying by instruments alone, the first course beginning in September 1931. Fitted with blind-flying hoods and Reid and Sigrist turn indicators, they had 1° less dihedral to reduce their inherent stability. This C.F.S. aircraft (below) was photographed over Wittering in June 1931, during trials.

Armstrong Whitworth Atlas

The two-seat Armstrong Whitworth Atlas was the first aircraft to enter RAF service which was designed from the outset for army co-operation, a role previously performed by specially modified Bristol Fighters. The prototype first flew in May 1925 and entered RAF service with the re-formed No 26 Squadron at Catterick, Yorkshire in October 1927. Overseas, the Atlas served with No 208 Squadron in Egypt from early 1930.

Powered by a 450-hp Armstrong Siddeley Jaguar IVC the Atlas had a top speed of 142 mph at sea level and was armed with a fixed Vickers gun forward and a free Lewis on a Scarff ring-mounting aft. It was eventually supplanted by the Hawker Audax after a total of 446 had been built, this figure including 175 dual-control Atlas trainers, which entered service from 1931.

The aircraft shown here are from No 4 (Army Co-operation) Squadron, Farnborough, photographed in July 1930.

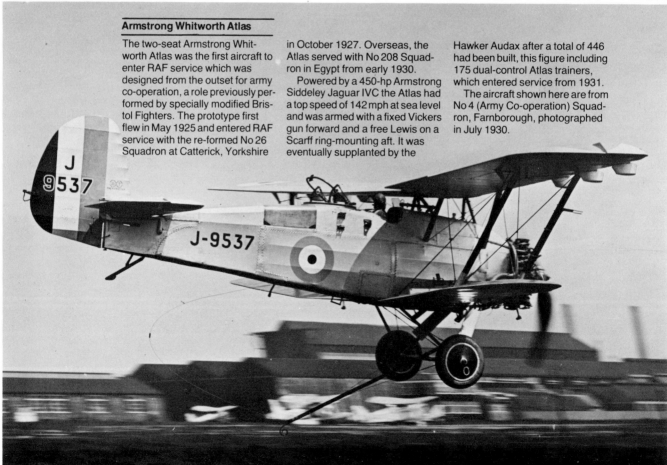

Fairey IIIF

A two-seat 'General Purpose' aircraft, the Fairey IIIF first re-equipped No 47 Squadron in Khartoum in 1927, replacing the squadron's aged Bristol Fighters. Apart from the Hawker Hart variants, the IIIF was built in greater numbers than any other British military aircraft between the two World Wars until the Hawker Hurricane was ordered in 1936, although the majority was destined for Fleet Air Arm service in its three-seat form. In RAF service the IIIF made many notable long-distance flights, amongst which were the Cairo to Cape Town flights of 1927, 1928 and 1929 by No 47 Squadron and the 1930 Cairo to Cape Town flight by No 14 Squadron. In Britain, the type was used as a day bomber, first equipping No 207 Squadron at Eastchurch in January 1928, and later going to No 35 Squadron at Bircham Newton. It was powered by a 570-hp Napier Lion XIA engine and carried a bomb load of 500 lb. Maximum speed was 120 mph.

Fairey IIIF, S1320, (above) was photographed in April 1929. Also illustrated is J9 154, with a Rolls-Royce Jaguar VI engine.

Boulton and Paul Sidestrand

Although it equipped only one squadron, No 101 at Bircham Newton in Norfolk, the Boulton and Paul Sidestrand was nevertheless significant because it was the first RAF aircraft to be designated as a medium bomber. The Sidestrand I prototype first flew in 1926 and the type entered service in April 1928. Powered by a pair of 460-hp Bristol Jupiter VIIIF engines the Sidestrand had a top speed of 140 mph at 10,000 ft. It was an extremely aerobatic aeroplane for its size (spanning almost 72 ft and weighing more than 10,000 lb fully loaded), an attribute amply demonstrated at the Hendon Air Displays of 1929, 1932 and 1933. Eighteen production aircraft were built and the type was superseded by the Overstrand in December 1934.

This formation of No 101 Squadron aircraft (above) was photographed over Andover in April 1931, while Sidestrand III, J9186, is significant because it was later to become the Overstrand prototype. (see page 59)

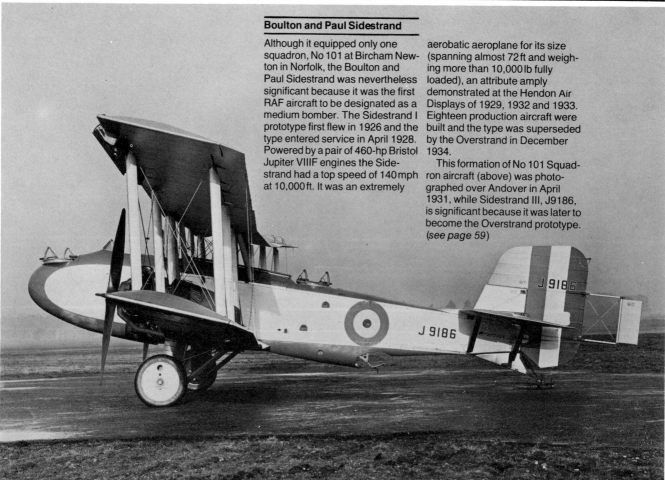

1929~1938

Bristol Bulldog

Captain Frank Barnwell's superb Bristol Bulldog interceptor fighter was adopted by the RAF after comparative trials with no less than nine types, and this Gamecock and Siskin replacement first entered service with No 3 Squadron at Upavon in June 1929. Altogether 312 Bulldogs were built for the RAF, the first forty-eight being designated Mk II and the remainder Mk IIA. Principal differences between the two Marks were a strengthened structure, increased loaded weight, redesigned oil system and revised undercarriage on the IIA. Later changes included a modified fin and a tailwheel in place of the original skid. The Bulldog was powered by the 490-hp Bristol Jupiter VIIF engine on which it could manage a top speed of 178mph at 10,000 ft, and armament was a pair of synchronised Vickers machine guns on either side of the nose.

By 1932 Bulldogs equipped nine squadrons and for some years they comprised about 70 per cent of British fighter defences, the last aircraft being replaced by Gladiators in 1937.

Both photographs show aircraft from No 17 Squadron, photographed in June 1930.

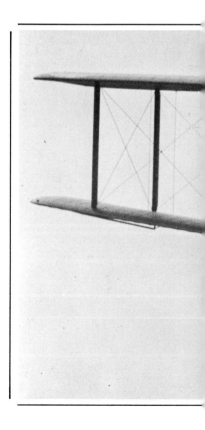

Handley Page Hinaidi

The Handley Page Hinaidi bomber was a development of the Hyderabad, which it closely resembled, and differed principally in being of all-metal construction and in having a pair of 440-hp Bristol Jupiter VIII engines in place of the Hyderabad's Lions. With a maximum speed of 122 mph at sea level and carrying a bomb load of 1,448 lb its performance was only marginally better than that of the Hyderabad. It first entered service with No 99 Squadron at Upper Heyford, Oxfordshire, in October 1929; later it equipped No 10 Squadron at Upper Heyford and Nos 502 and 503 Squadrons, Auxiliary Air Force. It was declared obsolete in 1937, No 99 Squadron having swapped its Hinaidis for Heyfords as early as 1933.

Westland Wapiti

The Westland Wapiti two-seat general purpose aircraft was the winner of a competition to find a replacement for the D.H.9A and in its original form used many 'Nine-Ack' components. Introduced in 1931, it saw considerable service on the North-West Frontier of India and in Iraq, being used for such diverse tasks as Army co-operation with message hooks and bombing. During the evacuation of Kabul in December 1928 and early 1929, Wapitis of No 20 Squadron escorted No 70 Squadron's Victoria troop carriers through the Khyber Pass to Peshawar.

Powered by a 480-hp Bristol Jupiter VIII engine, the all-metal Wapiti IIA had a top speed of 140 mph at 5,000 ft. Total Wapiti production for the RAF amounted to 512, ending in 1932. In the UK, Wapitis served mainly with the Auxiliary Air Force and were not retired until 1937. In India about eighty Wapitis remained in RAF service at least until the outbreak of the Second World War. Shown below are four Wapiti IIAs of No 601 Squadron over Lympne in August 1930. Left: this line-up of Wapitis in India is of No 31 Squadron's aircraft, while K1132, (below) photographed in September 1930, shows an aircraft equipped with special fuel tanks used for long distance desert patrol work.

Hawker Hart

The Hawker Hart was one of Sydney Camm's masterpieces, and more aircraft of Hart origin were built between the two World Wars than of any other basic design in Great Britain. Designated a two-seat light day bomber, it was chosen after competitive trials with the Fairey Fox II and the Avro Antelope. The first fifteen development aircraft were delivered to No 33 Squadron at Eastchurch in January 1930, and this squadron, which had previously been equipped with Horsleys, was able to achieve second place in the annual Bomber Command inter-unit contest within three months. Sub-variants included the Hart (C) for communications duties, the Hart (India), which first flew in September 1931, and the Hart (Special), which was an Audax airframe modified to take desert equipment, a tropical radiator, a braked undercarriage with heavy-duty tyres and a de-rated Rolls-Royce Kestrel X engine.

Between 1930 and 1936, seven home-based squadrons of the regular RAF flew Harts and from March 1933 it entered service with the Auxiliary Air Force, equipping eight squadrons. Overseas, Harts were to be found in Egypt and Palestine as well as in India where they began replacing Wapitis in November 1931. By 1936, the Hart was being replaced by the Hind in home-based light bomber squadrons, but on the North-West Frontier of India some Harts were still operating as late as 1939, when they were replaced by Blenheims.

Performance was excellent, maximum speed being 184 mph at 5,000 ft, a figure which caused some consternation during the 1930 Air Exercises since the intercepting Siskins were unable to catch the attacking Harts. Some advantage was to come of this, however, since it probably accelerated development of the Fury fighter.

This formation of No 57 Squadron Harts (below) was photographed in June 1934 during rehearsals for that year's Hendon Air Display. Above: the immaculately dressed line-up is of early Hart Trainers.

Fairey Gordon

Like the Fleet Air Arm's Seal, the Fairey Gordon two-seat day bomber and general purpose aircraft was a derivative of the Fairey IIIF, and in its prototype from was known as the IIIF Mk V. It first flew in March 1931 and entered service with No 40 Squadron at Upper Heyford in April 1931. Powered by the uncowled 525-hp Armstrong Siddeley Panther IIA fourteen-cylinder two-row radial engine, the Gordon could manage a top speed of 145 mph at 3,000 ft and carried a bomb-load of 460 lb. Because of the diameter of the engine the foward-firing Vickers gun had to be mounted externally, on the left-hand side of the fuselage, although the IIIF-type Fairey high-speed mounting was retained for the aft-firing Lewis. The Gordon remained in front-line service at home and overseas until as late as 1938 and some were operating at air armament schools for gunnery target drogue towing at the outbreak of the Second World War in September 1939.

The formation is of No 40 Squadron aircraft, while K2617 (below) is one of No 6 Squadron's Gordons, seen here at Ismailia, Egypt.

Hawker Demon

The Hawker Demon was a two-seat version of the extremely successful Hart, the prototype in fact being a converted Hart bomber with fully supercharged Rolls-Royce Kestrel IIS, twin front guns and a cutaway rear cockpit with a tilted gun-ring to provide a better field of fire for the observer/gunner. Hart fighters – re-named Demon in July 1932 – were issued to one flight of No 23 Squadron at Kenley

in March 1931 and in the Air Exercises of July of that year the Hart fighters showed themselves capable of intercepting their bomber counterparts. The first production Demon was flown in February 1933, and by April No 23 Squadron had converted entirely to Demons, replacing their Bulldogs.

From October 1936, all Demons built by Boulton Paul were fitted with a Fraser-Nash hydraulically-

operated turret with a 'lobster back' shield to protect the rear gunner from the effects of slipstream; these aircraft were known as Turret Demons and many other aircraft were retrospectively modified.

Demons served with eleven home fighter squadrons and four overseas squadrons, but by September the type had been declared obsolete and replaced in all oper-

ational squadrons. A small number continued to be used as target tugs until replaced by Henleys.

Demon K5721 (below), with the observer's gun trained on the photographer, is from No 601 Squadron, based at Hendon. Above: Demon I, K2857, has been converted for target-towing, and is seen here minus guns in its distinctive paint scheme.

Hawker Fury I

The Hawker Fury epitomized the biplane fighter of the 1930s: small, light, fast and possessing an outstanding rate of climb. Added to which it was, to most eyes, one of the most elegant aeroplanes of all time. Powered by the 525-hp Rolls-Royce Kestrel IIS, the Fury turned in a maximum speed of 207 mph at 14,000 ft, the first RAF fighter in squadron service to exceed 200 mph. Armament was a pair of synchronised Vickers guns installed in the top decking of the nose.

The first squadron to receive the Fury I was No 43 at Tangmere, Sussex, in May and June 1931, and in the annual Air Exercises of that year No 43 Squadron's Furies showed themselves to be easily the fastest aircraft participating.

During the winter of 1931-32 No 25 Squadron at Hawkinge, Kent, re-equipped with Furies, followed in May 1932 by the third and last Fury squadron, No 1 at Tangmere. The three squadrons were to give countless demonstrations of precision aerobatics and air drill both at home and overseas until the late 1930s.

Dominating the previous page is a Fury of No 25 Squadron, with a line-up of the Squadron's aircraft inset. Left: these No 1 Squadron Furies flying in echelon formation were practising for their goodwill tour of Switzerland in 1937.

Hawker Audax

Another Hart derivative, the Hawker Audax was the result of an Air Ministry requirement for an Armstrong Whitworth Atlas replacement. Externally it was distinguishable from the Hart by means of its message collecting hook on the undercarriage spreader bar, and by the extended exhaust pipes. Standard Hart armament of a single Vickers gun forward and Lewis gun on the observer's cockpit was retained.

The first Atlas squadron to be re-equipped was No 4 Squadron, based at Farnborough, in February 1932. Production for the RAF totalled 624 and ended in 1937. Home-based army co-operation squadrons were re-equipped with Hectors in 1937-38. Overseas, however, Audaxes were operational well into the Second World War, while at home some Audaxes were converted into glider tugs, serving at Kidlington, Croughton and Wellesbourne Mountford, towing Hotspur gliders.

Avro Tutor

The Avro Tutor succeeded Avro 504Ns in RAF Flying Training Schools from 1932, but was preceeded by a trial batch of Mongoose-engined Avro Trainers. The Mongoose Trainers entered service in 1930 and were used by the Air Navigation School at Andover from 1935 until their final withdrawal in 1937. The Lynx-engined Tutor entered service at the RAF College, Cranwell and No 5 Flying Training School, Sealand in 1933. Later, it became standard equipment at all flying training schools and with the University Air Squadrons until 1939.

At the 1933 Hendon Air Display six Tutors of the Central Flying School gave a display of aerobatics and inverted formation flying that became a regular feature of the show. Three are seen (below) practising, in June 1937. The upper surfaces of the wings were painted with red and white sunburst stripes to assist recognition by the spectators when the aircraft were inverted. Above: Tutor K6100, photographed some time in 1941, has had its rear cockpit blanked off.

Saunders-Roe Cloud

The Saro Cloud was originally built for civil use as a slightly larger version of the four-passenger Cutty Sark and first flew in 1931. In RAF service is was used for instruction of flying boat crews before they graduated to larger boats, and as a 'flying classroom' for training navigators. It first entered service with B Flight of the Seaplane Training Squadron at Calshot in August 1933. In addition to Calshot, the amphibian Cloud was also issued to the School of Air Pilotage at Andover and, in February 1935, to No 48 Squadron at Bircham Newton. Total production was sixteen aircraft, the last of which was delivered in June 1935.

Powered by a pair of 430-hp Armstrong Siddely Serval (Double Mongoose) engines, the Cloud had a maximum speed of 118mph and cruised at 95mph. They are seen here at Calshot in late 1933.

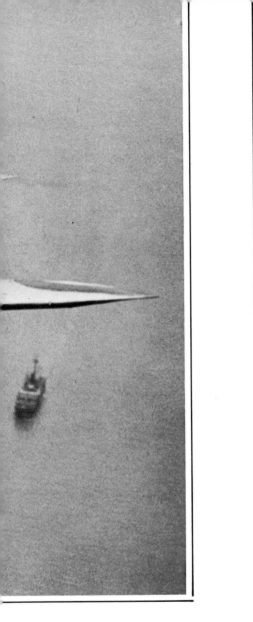

Vickers Vildebeest

The all-metal Vickers Vildebeest torpedo bomber was designed to replace the Hawker Horsley and first entered service with No 100 Squadron at Donibristle in 1933. Because of a delay in the introduction of Beauforts, Vildebeests were the only front-line torpedo bombers available to Coastal Command at the outbreak of the Second World War, and in the Far East two Vildebeest squadrons were left to face the Japanese invasion of Singapore in 1941.

The Vildebeest Mk II introduced the 660-hp Bristol Pegasus IIM$_3$ and the Mk III incorporated a permanent third crew member; total production of Marks I to III for the RAF was 176, ending in September 1936. The Vildebeest Mk IV was fitted with a 825-hp Bristol Perseus VIII sleeve-valve engine driving a Rotol three-blade variable-pitch propeller. Maximum speed of the Mark III was 143 mph and that of the Mk IV a respectable 156 mph. Armament was a fixed Vickers gun forward and a Lewis gun aft and 1,000 lb of bombs or a single 18-in torpedo.

Handley Page Heyford

Last of the RAF's biplane heavy bombers, the Handley Page Heyford was unusual in that the slim fuselage was attached to the upper wing instead of the lower, as in most other biplanes. This brought the lower wing closer to the ground, facilitating re-arming as the bomb load was carried in the thick centre section. The first squadron to receive Heyfords was No 99 Squadron at Upper Heyford, in November 1933. The type followed the Virginia into service in Nos 7, 9 and 10 Squadrons and was also issued to four new squadrons formed under the RAF expansion scheme. From 1937, Heyfords began to be withdrawn from operational use, the last front-line aircraft being replaced by Wellingtons in 1939. In the early part of the war some Heyfords were still being used for training and the type was not finally declared obsolete until July 1941.

Powered by a pair of 575-hp Rolls-Royce Kestrel IIIS engines, the Heyford IA had a top speed of 142 mph at 13,000 ft. It carried a crew of four and bomb load varied between 1,660 lb and 3,500 lb.

Shown to advantage (above) is the unusual arrangement of the wings on this Heyford of 'A' Flight, No 10 Squadron, July 1935. The formation photograph (top) is also of No 10 Squadron aircraft, probably taken at the same time. The occasion was King George V's Silver Jubilee review of the RAF (right).

Blackburn Perth

Succeeding the earlier Iris into service, the Blackburn Perth was originally known as the Iris VI and was the largest biplane flying boat ever used by the RAF. Only four of these long-range reconnaissance flying boats were built, the first of which was delivered to No 209 Squadron at Mount Batten in January 1934. The squadron was brought up to strength when the third aircraft was delivered at the end of May 1934. The fourth Perth, modified to carry only two gravity fuel tanks instead of the usual three, was nominally on No 209 Squadron's charge but spent its entire service life with 'A' Flight at the MAEE (Marine Aircraft Experimental Establishment) at Felixstowe, and was finally struck off charge in February 1938. Of the other three, one was lost off Stornoway in September 1935 without loss of life and the others were struck off charge in 1936, being replaced by the Short Singapore.

Powered by three 825-hp Rolls-Royce Buzzard IIMS engines, the Perth was capable of a maximum speed of 132 mph at sea level. It carried a crew of five and in addition to its conventional armament of .303-in machine guns was fitted with a bow station for the 37-mm Coventry Ordnance Works anti-shipping cannon on a manually-operated Vickers-Westland mounting. This well-known photograph shows the second Perth, K3581, over the coast of Cornwall in 1934.

Short Singapore III

The Short Singapore III general reconnaissance flying boat, which first entered service with No 230 Squadron at Pembroke Dock in April 1935, was the final Service version of a design which originated with the twin Rolls-Royce H 10-engined Singapore I of 1926. The Singapore II did not go into production and the first Mark III flew in June 1934, production ending in 1937 after a total of thirty-seven had been built for the RAF. Singapore IIIs equipped six squadrons at home and a further two abroad. By the outbreak of war in 1939, some nineteen Singapore IIIs in full camouflage remained in service and No 205 Squadron, based at Singapore, still had four aircraft on strength as late as December 1941.

Powered by four 560-hp Rolls-Royce Kestrel IIIMS and IIMS engines mounted back-to-back in pairs, the Singapore had a top speed of 145 mph at 2,000 ft and an endurance of more than six hours. Singapore III K3582, seen here at Pembroke in January 1935, is one of No 210 Squadron's aircraft.

Gloster Gauntlet

The open-cockpit Gloster Gauntlet has tended to be overshadowed by the better-known Gladiator, but in its hey-day during the late 1930s the type equipped some fourteen Fighter Command squadrons and was the fastest fighter in service with a top speed of 230 mph. Gauntlet Is first equipped No 19 Squadron at Duxford in May 1935, a total of twenty-four of that Mark being built. The Gauntlet II, of which some 204 were ordered, featured a new type of wing spar and rear fuselage construction and first deliveries of this Mark went to Northolt in May 1936 for distribution between No 56 and 111 Squadrons. The last squadron to be equipped was No 74 'Tiger' Squadron based at Hornchurch, during 1937. During 1938, most of the Gauntlet Is were withdrawn from home-based front-line squadrons and three-bladed Fairey propellers were introduced on most of the Mark IIs. Gladiators and Hurricanes were then entering service, but it was not until 1939 that the last Gauntlets left Fighter Command; in September 1939 there were still twenty-six of the type serving with four Auxiliary Air Force squadrons, with a further forty-five aircraft in the Middle East where some continued to fly well into 1940.

The superb formation photograph on the previous pages is of No 19 Squadron's Gauntlets.

Supermarine Scapa

Originally known as the Southampton IV, the Supermarine Scapa general reconnaissance flying boat first flew in 1932. Carrying a crew of five, the all-metal Scapa was powered by two 525-hp Rolls-Royce Kestrel IIIMS engines which gave it a top speed of 141 mph at 3,000 ft. It was aerodynamically more refined than the Southampton, particularly around the wing centre section and in the method of fairing its neatly cowled Rolls-Royce engines into the upper wing, and this was reflected in its superior performance.

Scapas first joined No 202 Squadron in Malta in May 1935 and were withdrawn from there in November 1937. At home, they first entered service with 204 Squadron at Mount Batten in August 1935, subsequently serving in Egypt during the Abyssinian crisis. The Scapa was finally withdrawn from front-line squadrons in 1938.

This photograph of K4200 at Southampton in November 1935 shows the neatness of the engine installation. Also visible is the top of the enclosed cockpit, another improvement over the spartan Supermarine Southampton.

Boulton Paul Overstrand

The Boulton Paul Overstrand five-seat medium bomber was a fairly straightforward development of the earlier Bristol Jupiter-engined Sidestrand. In fact, the prototype, which first flew in 1933, was a converted Sidestrand fitted with two 580-hp Bristol Pegasus IIM3 engines and a power-operated enclosed gun turret in the nose, the Overstrand being the first RAF aircraft to carry one. Other significant improvements included an enclosed cockpit for the pilot, automatic pilot and heating for the crew. The first unit to be equipped with the Overstrand was No 101 Squadron, in 1934. This was the only squadron to operate the aircraft as a front-line bomber and continued to fly the Overstrand until 1937, when they converted to the new Blenheim monoplane. Top speed was 153 mph at 6,500 ft and bomb load a maximum of 1,600 lb. Only twenty-four were built, all at the old Boulton Paul factory at Norwich.

Overstrand J9186 (below) was the first prototype. Compare this photograph with that on page 40. Another converted Sidestrand was J9185 (left), photographed in January 1935.

Hawker Hardy

Another variant of the prolific Hart family, the Hawker Hardy was a two-seat general purpose type for service in the Middle East. Generally similar to the Audax, it was fitted with more diverse equipment for its specific 'policing' role, including tropical survival kit, water containers, message pick-up hook and tropical radiator. First flight was in September 1934 and the type first entered service with No 30 Squadron, based at Mosul in Iraq, where it replaced the squadron's veteran Wapitis. No 6 Squadron in Palestine also operated Hardys, receiving No 30 Squadron's aircraft in 1938, low-pressure tyres being fitted to facilitate operation from desert landing strips. At the outbreak of war the remaining Hardy's were turned over to No 237 (Rhodesia) Squadron, finally being withdrawn after the Battle of Karen. A total of forty-seven aircraft was built.

First Gloster-built Hardy, K4050 was fitted with the 530-hp Rolls-Royce Kestrel IB engine. It was photographed at Hucklecote in September 1934.

Carrying bombs under the lower wings and a Lewis gun in the observer's cockpit, Hardy K4315 (below) on patrol in Palestine. Noticeable are the large low-pressure tyres.

Hawker Hind

The Hawker Hind light bomber was essentially an interim replacement for the Hart during the early part of the RAF expansion scheme, while the Service was waiting for the new generation of monoplane bombers. Powered by the 640-hp Rolls-Royce Kestrel V engine, the Hind had a top speed of 186 mph at 16,400 ft and carried the same bomb load of 500 lb as the earlier Hart. Apart from the considerably more powerful engine, the Hind also benefited from improved accommodation for the observer/gunner in the prone bomb-aiming position and the rear cockpit was cut away in much the same way as that on the Demon. The prototype Hind first flew in September 1934 and production aircraft began equipping Nos 18, 21 and 34 Squadrons at Bircham Newton in Norfolk during November 1935. At the peak of its career in 1937 no fewer than twenty bomber squadrons of the RAF were equipped with Hinds, together with a further seven Auxiliary Air Force squadrons.

These Hinds of No 50 Squadron were photographed near Waddington in May 1938.

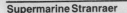

Supermarine Stranraer

The twin-engined Supermarine Stranraer six-seat general reconnaissance flying boat first entered service with No 338 Squadron at Pembroke Dock in 1936, later equipping Nos 201, 209 and 240 Squadrons. The Stranraer saw no overseas service during its time with Coastal Command and was finally withdrawn in 1940 with the arrival of the accident-prone Lerwick at 209 Squadron and the infinitely more successful Sunderland at No 201 Squadron. Last of the biplane flying boats designed by R.J. Mitchell, the Stranraer was originally designated the Southampton Mk V but was renamed in August 1935. Total orders were for twenty-three aircraft. Powered by two 875-hp Bristol Pegasus X radial engines, the Stranraer had a top speed of 165 mph at 6,000 ft and an endurance of more than six and a half hours.

Avro Anson I

The Avro Anson, 'Faithful Annie', must be one of the longest serving military aircraft of all time. It first entered service with No 48 Squadron at Manston on March 6, 1936 and the six surviving Ansons were finally retired from the Southern Communications Squadron at Bovingdon on June 28, 1968. Although the Anson served with front-line Coastal Command squadrons from its introduction in 1936 until the opening stages of the war as a coastal reconnaissance aircraft, it spent most of its service life employed as a navigation trainer and general communications aircraft. Total production of the Anson I in Britain was just under 7,000, some of the later ones being converted for communications and air ambulance duties. After the war the RAF took delivery of an improved transport version, the C.19, and a new navigation trainer, the T.21, with metal wings and tailplane.

These two photographs are of Anson Is; the formation is of aircraft from No 217 Squadron, Coastal Command.

Saunders-Roe London

The Saro London six-seat general reconnaissance flying boat first went into service with No 204 Squadron, Mount Batten, in October 1936, replacing the Squadron's Southamptons of 1925 vintage. At the outbreak of war, in September 1939, the RAF had twenty-nine of the type, and in Gibraltar No 202 Squadron was operating its Londons until 1941. For the 1937-38 cruise from the UK to New South Wales, Australia, and back, No 204 Squadron's Londons were equipped with a special long-range fuel tank increasing the range to 2,600 miles from the nominal 1,100 miles. Powered by two 1,000-hp Bristol Pegasus X radial engines, the London II had a top speed of 155 mph at 6,250 ft and cruised at 129 mph.

The London IIs in these photographs were all converted from London Mk Is. The airborne pair were photographed at Calshot in December 1937.

Fairey Hendon

The Fairey Hendon was notable as the first of the RAF's all-metal cantilever monoplane heavy bombers to go into squadron service, equipping No 38 Squadron at Mildenhall, Suffolk, in November 1936, replacing the squadron's Heyfords. No 38 Squadron was the only unit to be equipped completely with Hendons; No 115 Squadron at Marham was formed from the detachment of one flight of Hendons from No 38 Squadron. The type remained in service until replaced by Wellingtons in July 1939. Total production was only fourteen aircraft, an additional contract for sixty being cancelled.

The Hendon II (the production version) carried a crew of five and was powered by a pair of 600-hp Rolls-Royce Kestrel IV engines which gave it a top speed of only 155 mph at 15,000 ft. Maximum bomb load was 1,660 lb.

K5093 of No 38 Squadron is seen taking off at Marham in late May, 1938.

Handley Page Harrow

Although designated a heavy bomber with a crew of five, the Handley Page Harrow was not destined to see operational service in that role since all Harrow squadrons had converted to Wellingtons by the outbreak of war. Instead it was decided to use the type on transport duties, a gentle irony since that was the role for which it had originally been designed. The first Harrow bomber squadron to be equipped was No 214 Squadron at Feltwell, in January 1937. Four other squadrons, Nos 37, 75, 115 and 215, received their Harrow bombers during 1937.

With its withdrawal as a bomber in 1939, some Harrows were converted for the transport role by the removal of the gun turrets and some modification of the nose. In this form it could carry twenty troops or an equivalent load in freight.

Photographed at Radlett at the end of March 1937 was this Harrow I in its bomber form.

Hawker Hector

The Hawker Hector two-seat Army Co-operation aircraft differed from other Hart variants principally in having the slim in-line Rolls-Royce Kestrel replaced by the unusual 24-cylinder 805-hp Napier Dagger IIIMS engine with its cylinders arranged in an 'H' cross-section, and by having a straight upper wing to compensate for the shift in centre-of-gravity which resulted from the introduction of the heavier engine. The prototype first flew in February 1936 and the first production aircraft, built by Westland at Yeovil, flew in February 1937, the same month that deliveries began to No 4 (Army Co-operation) Squadron at Odiham. By the end of the year five home-based army co-operation squadrons had been equipped with Hectors, with a further two in 1938. By the end of 1938, however, Westland's Lysander began to supplant Hectors in front-line service and the older aircraft were issued to Auxiliary Air Force squadrons. AAF Hectors saw some action in the early part of the war, but for the majority that survived into 1941 their swansong was to be as glider tugs, towing Hotspur troop training light gliders at Wellesbourne Mountford, Croughton and Kidlington.

Both aircraft shown here were photographed in 1937: K8108 (above) is a No 13 Squadron aircraft from Odiham, while the other is from No 615 Squadron, Kenley.

Hawker Fury II

The Hawker Fury II was built as an interim replacement for the Fury I before the new monoplane Hurricane entered large-scale squadron service. The design was based on the Intermediate and High-Speed Furies and the Fury II was powered by the 640-hp Rolls-Royce Kestrel VI which gave it a top speed of 223 mph at 16,400 ft. More dramatic, perhaps, than the eight per cent increase in speed over the Fury I was the thirty-four per cent increase in rate of climb, a notable asset in an interceptor fighter.

The first production Fury II flew in December 1936 and deliveries to No 25 Squadron at Hawkinge began early the following year, replacing the squadron's Fury Is. Subsequently Nos 41, 43, 87 and 73 Squadrons were all issued with Fury IIs, but these had been replaced by Gladiators, Hurricanes and Spitfires by 1939. Total production amounted to 108 aircraft, a small number of which was shipped to South Africa in 1938.

Photographed in late April 1933, K3586 was the High-Speed Fury, fitted with the Rolls-Royce Kestrel VIS and tapered wing with vee interplane struts. K7284 (below) was a standard Fury II with N-type interplane struts.

Gloster Gladiator

The single-seat Gloster Gladiator marked the end of the era of the RAF's fighter biplanes and although already obsolete by the outbreak of the Second World War it had a distinguished, if sometimes tragic, wartime career. A development of H.P. Folland's Gauntlet, the 840-hp Bristol Mercury IX-engined fighter had a top speed of 253 mph at 14,500 ft. Armament was four .303-in Browning machine guns, two mounted on the lower wing and firing outside the propeller arc, and a further two mounted either side of the nose.

The first Gladiators entered service with No 72 Squadron in February 1937, followed by No 3 Squadron in March. By the outbreak of war, thirteen of Fighter Command's thirty-five squadrons were still flying Gladiators and two of these, Nos 607 and 615, were sent to France as part of the Advanced Air Striking Force. The most celebrated wartime exploits of the Gladiator were almost exclusively overseas: No 263 Squadron in Norway; Nos 33, 80, 94 and 112 Squadrons against the Italian Air Force in the Western Desert; and the defence of Malta. Photographed in late June 1935, K5200 was the prototype G.37 Gladiator.

Bristol Blenheim I

The Bristol Blenheim I light bomber was marginally faster than the RAF's contemporary biplane fighters when it entered service, with No 114 Squadron at Wyton, in March 1937 and it remained the Service's fastest light bomber for some time. It had its genesis in Frank Barnwell's Bristol Type 142, built for Lord Rothermere, presented to the Nation by the owner and whimsically called 'Britain First'. This aircraft had such excellent performance that the Air Ministry ordered 150 'off the drawing board' and the name Blenheim was conferred on the type. Powered by two 840-hp Bristol Mercury VIII engines, the Blenheim I had a top speed of 260 mph and carried a maximum bomb load of 1,000 lb; armament was a forward-firing .303-in Browning machine gun in the port wing and a Vickers 'K' gun in a hydraulically-operated dorsal turret. By the outbreak of war it had been superseded by the Blenheim IV in most home-based bomber squadrons but a few saw operational service in the Western Desert and Greece. As the Blenhiem IF night-fighter, however, it saw extensive service. Armament was augmented by four .303-in Brownings in a gun-pack below the fuselage and the aircraft was fitted with an early version of Airborne Interception (AI) radar.

This Blenheim I, K7059, from No 90 Squadron, Bicester, was photographed in November 1938 with its semi-retracting dorsal turret in the fully-extended position.

Vickers Wellesley

The Vickers Wellesley two-seat general-purpose bomber was the first RAF aircraft to use the radical geodetic construction method developed for airships by Barnes Wallis. Built as a private venture development of the Pegasus-engined G.4/31 biplane, the prototype Wellesley first flew in June 1935. Performance margin over the biplane was such that the Air Ministry switched contracts to the new monoplane, the first production aircraft flying in January 1937. First squadron to be equipped with the Wellesley was No 76 at Finningly, which received the first of its aircraft in April 1937. Within a year, Nos 35, 207, 77 and 148 Squadrons of Bomber Command were similarly equipped and shortly afterwards the first Wellesley were equipping overseas squadrons.

The Wellesley is best remembered as the aircraft which broke the World Long-Distance Record. In 1938 five aircraft were allotted to the Long Range Development Unit, modifications including provision of extra fuel tankage, new Rotol constant-speed propellers and introduction of the Mk IV automatic pilot. On November 5, 1938 three Wellesleys, led by Squadron Leader R. Kellett took off from Ismailia, Egypt, to fly non-stop to Darwin, Australia. One aircraft landed prematurely at Kupang, Timor, because of lack of fuel, but the remaining two reached Darwin after forty-eight hours in the air having covered more than 7,000 miles, a record that stood for eight years.

de Havilland Tiger Moth

The first thirty-five examples of this outstanding training biplane reached the RAF in February 1932, being distributed to the Central Flying School and other flying training schools. At the 1932 Hendon Air Display, the CFS used five for inverted formation flying. In 1934 the Air Ministry ordered fifty improved Tiger Moths fitted with 130-hp Gipsy Major engines, ply decking on the rear fuselage and a blind-flying hood for the rear cockpit. Known as the Tiger Moth II, this became the definitive trainer version for the RAF. By the outbreak of war more than 1,000 had been delivered, the majority serving in the Elementary and Reserve Flying Training Schools, providing *ab initio* instruction for pilots before they graduated to the Service Flying Training Schools. During the war they equipped no fewer than twenty-eight Reserve and Elementary Flying Schools in Britain, as well as fifty-five overseas. Total production by August 1945 exceeded 8,000, of which more than 6,200 were built in the UK.

The pre-war CFS display team is seen here (top) in characteristic formation in its Tiger Moth Is. Early Tiger Moth Is had traditional fabric-covered stringers on the fuselage top (centre), but later Mk IIs were ply-decked and incorporated strakes forward of the tail plane to assist in spin recovery. Below: EM836, a Tiger Moth II, is being fitted with 25-lb Cooper bombs for use against a possible German invasion early in the war.

Armstrong Whitworth Whitley

Classified as a long-range night bomber, the Armstrong Whitworth Whitley was one of the mainstays of the poorly equipped Bomber Command in the early stages of the war, and bore the brunt of the leaflet raids over Germany that were known by the code-name 'Nickel'. The prototype Whitley made its first flight in March 1936 and the first Whitley Mk Is began to equip No 10 Squadron in March 1937. The Whitley II, the first of which were delivered in January 1938, was the first RAF aircraft to be equipped with a two-stage supercharger and the Mk III, delivered in August 1938, differed from other variants in being fitted with a ventral 'dustbin' gun turret. Major production variant was the Rolls-Royce Merlin X-engined Whitley V, some 1,466 of which were built between 1939 and 1943. A Coastal Command variant known as the G.R. VII was built in parallel with the Mk Vs and, equipped with ASV radar and increased fuel tankage, was used for anti-submarine patrol. A G.R. VII from No 502 Squadron made Coastal Command's first U-boat 'kill' by sinking U-206 in the Bay of Biscay on November 30, 1941. Whitleys also made valuable contributions as glider tugs and parachute trainers and for their work with the Special Duties No 100 Group.

Fairey Battle

The Fairey Battle light bomber was a tragic aeroplane. Designed as a replacement for the Hart and Hind biplane bombers, it looked marvellous when it first appeared in 1936, carrying twice the bomb load twice as far and at fifty per cent higher speed. Powered by the excellent Rolls-Royce Merlin it was, however, underpowered and hopelessly lacking in defensive firepower and within four years of its first public appearance it was to be shot out of the sky by marauding German fighters.

Battles first entered service with No 63 Squadron at Upwood, Huntingdon, in May 1937 and just over a year later they equipped fifteen Bomber Command squadrons. By the outbreak of war, there were more than 1,000 in service, although the type had been accepted as obsolescent. After several disastrous encounters with enemy fighters the Battle was withdrawn from front-line service and by the end of 1940 was largely employed in training duties. Armament was a single forward firing Browning machine gun and a Vickers 'K' gun aft. Total production amounted to more than 2,400 of which about 800 were sent to Canada for use under the Commonwealth Air Training Plan; a further 400 were shipped to Australia.

Fairey Battle I, K7558, was the first production aircraft, seen here in August 1937.

Airspeed Oxford

The Airspeed Oxford was the RAF's first twin-engined monoplane advanced trainer and entered service with the Central Flying School in November 1937. A military development of the civil Envoy, the prototype Oxford first flew in June 1937 and by the outbreak of war nearly 400 had been delivered. Known to crews as the 'Ox-Box' the Oxford I was originally intended for all aspects of crew training, including gunnery for which an Armstrong Whitworth dorsal turret was fitted. The Oxford II was used mainly for pilot training and had the turret removed. By the end of the war the staggering total of 8,586 had been built.

After the war the type was used for communications duties until the requirement for National Service pilots created a new demand for multi-engine trainers. They were finally withdrawn from service in 1954 with the closure of No 10 Advanced Flying Training School at Pershore.

Right: AS592 was the 'Oxford V' prototype and was fitted with a pair of Pratt & Whitney Wasp Juniors.

Miles Magister

Affectionately known as the 'Maggie' the Miles Magister was the RAF's first monoplane trainer and was introduced in September 1937. Produced to meet the requirement for a new low-wing elementary trainer the Magister was faster than contemporary biplane trainers with a top speed of 132 mph yet had a landing speed of only 42 mph. Its design owed much to the series of civil light aircraft designed by F.G. Miles and was virtually indistinguishable from the Miles Hawk Trainer Mk III.

Left: N3780 was a Magister I, fitted with blind-flying hood over the rear cockpit and anti-spin strakes forward of the tailplane.

Hawker Hurricane I

The first of the eight-gun monoplane fighters, the Hawker Hurricane made its maiden flight on
November 6, 1935, powered by a
Rolls-Royce 'C' driving a Watts
two-blade fixed-pitch wooden
propeller. After handling trials had
been conducted at the Aircraft and
Armament Experimental Establishment at Martlesham Heath
early in 1936, a production order
for 600 aircraft was placed, the first
production Hurricane I flying in
October 1937.

The first RAF fighter squadron to
receive its Hurricanes was No 111
Squadron at Northolt in December
1937, which exchanged its
Gauntlets, followed by No 3
Squadron at Kenley, previously
equipped with Gladiators. At the
outbreak of war, Fighter Command
possessed nineteen full squadrons of Hurricanes, two of which,
Nos 1 and 73, flew to France with
the Advanced Air Striking Force, to
be joined by Nos 85 and 87 Squadrons of the Air Component. The
first enemy aircraft to be shot down
on the Western Front fell to the
guns of a No 1 Squadron Hurricane. By the beginning of the
Battle of Britain in August 1940,
some thirty-two Hurricane squadrons were available and during that
Battle, while Hurricanes were

shooting down more enemy aircraft than all other defences, air
and ground combined, average
strength of the type was running at
1,326, compared with 957 Spitfires.

Powered by the 1,030-hp
Rolls-Royce Merlin II, maximum
speed was 324 mph with the Rotol
three-bladed propeller. Up until the
middle of 1940, Hurricane production had been concentrated on
the basic Mk I, but in June 1940 the
prototype Hurricane IIA, powered
by a 1,185-hp Rolls-Royce Merlin XX engine (later rated at
1,280 hp) made its first flight.
Delivery to Fighter Command
squadrons began in August 1940.

Meanwhile, Hurricane Is were
being equipped with tropical air
filters prior to operating in the
Mediterranean and Middle East
theatres after the entry of Italy into
the war. At home, several Hurricane I squadrons were temporarily
withdrawn to train in night fighting
and before the end of 1940 they
would be engaged in the night
defence of London, alongside
Blenheims and Defiants.

Westland Lysander

The Westland Lysander replaced Hawker Hector biplane Army Co-operation aircraft in 1938, the first squadron to be re-equipped being No 16, based at Old Sarum in June of that year. Initially it was used for reconnaissance and artillery spotting but with the outbreak of war it was called upon to perform a variety of tasks, and the type is credited with the destruction of a Heinkel He III, shot down in BEF territory, in November 1939. The 'Lizzie' also served in the Western Desert, having been issued to No 208 Squadron in Egypt in April 1939. From 1941, home-based Lysanders were replaced in the army co-operation role by Tomahawks, but the type continued to serve as a target tug and on air-sea rescue duties.

A special version of the Lysander, known as the Lysander III(SCW), was used to transport Allied agents into enemy-occupied territory. Fitted with long-range tanks it had an endurance of eight hours and equipped Nos 138 and 161 Squadrons.

Supermarine Spitfire I

It has been written of the Supermarine Spitfire that it was more than just a highly successful fighter; it was the material symbol of final victory to the British people in their darkest hour, and it was probably the only fighter of the Second World War to achieve a truly legendary status. As originally conceived by the brilliant R.J. Mitchell, the private venture Supermarine Type 300 single-seat fighter was merely the smallest and simplest aeroplane that could be evolved around the Rolls-Royce PV-12 engine. The design was accepted by the Air Ministry in January 1935 for prototype construction to Specification F.37/34, and on March 5, 1936, the prototype Spitfire was flown, powered by the 990-hp Rolls-Royce Merlin C. From the start the Spitfire demonstrated that it was a classic aeroplane; it handled beautifully and was endowed with superlative performance.

Initial contracts for 310 aircraft were placed in June 1936, and these were completed by August 1939. The first squadron to be re-equipped with the new eight-gun Spitfire was No 19 Squadron at Duxford, in July 1938. The production Spitfire I differed from the prototype in having a 1,030-hp Merlin II engine, ejector exhausts and a tailwheel in place of the skid.

Early aircraft were fitted with a two-bladed fixed-pitch propeller, but this was later replaced by a de Havilland three-bladed variable-pitch type, and ultimately by a constant speed propeller. A new domed cockpit canopy and bullet-proof windscreen were also added to later Mk Is. The first aircraft were fitted with only four .303-in Brownings because of the acute gun shortage, but armament was later increased to eight in the Mk IA. In its definitive Mk I form, the Spitfire was capable of a top speed of 355 mph at 19,000 ft and could climb to 15,000 ft in 6¼ minutes.

By July 1940, Fighter Command had nineteen squadrons of Spitfires in readiness for the Battle of Britain, and during the period between mid-July and the end of October 1940 the average strength in Spitfires was 957, as against an average of 1,326 Hurricanes. More than 1,500 Spitfire Is were built, to be followed by 920 Mk IIs, which were fitted with the more powerful 1,175-hp Merlin XII engine. Armed with eight .303 machine guns (Mk IIA) or four .303 machine guns and two 20-mm cannon (Mk IIB), the new type first entered squadron service from August 1940 and was used in Fighter Command's early offensive sweeps over Europe.

Short Sunderland

The Short Sunderland flying boat has the distinction of being the longest-serving front-line aircraft to be operated by the RAF, from its introduction into No 230 Squadron in Singapore in the summer of 1938 to its eventual withdrawal from service in May 1959, when the last two aircraft of No 205 Squadron flew from Seletar for the last time.

Produced as a military development of the 'C' Class Empire flying boat, the Sunderland marked a vast improvement in armament and performance over previous biplane flying boats, being equipped with power-operated turrets in the bow and tail. Nicknamed by the Luftwaffe the 'Flying Porcupine' the Sunderland rapidly gained a fearsome reputation both for its ability to defend itself against enemy aircraft and for its success against U-boats. By the beginning of 1943 the Sunderland equipped nine Coastal Command squadrons, mainly in its Mk III

form, and the number of U-boat kills began to mount steadily.

Last variant to be built was the Mk V, which first entered service with No 228 Squadron in February 1945, powered by four 1,200-hp Pratt and Whitney Twin Wasp engines which gave the type a top speed of 213 mph at 5,000 ft. This variant, which was used in the Berlin Airlift, in Korea and against the terrorists in Malaya, remained in service until 1959.

These photographs show Sunderland M.R.5s at Pembroke Docks in 1955.

Handley Page Hampden

The curious looking Handley Page Hampden was one of the world's most advanced military aircraft when it first appeared in June 1936, having a relatively low landing speed by virtue of its well flapped and slatted wings and a respectably high maximum speed. In fact it was faster than its contemporaries the Whitley and Wellington, nearly as fast as the Blenhiem I light bomber and carried twice as many bombs twice as far. Its weakness, however, lay in its inadequate defensive armament, which comprised a fixed gun for the pilot and twin .303-in guns at the rear, above and below the fuselage. The limited traverse of these rear guns left a number of blind spots and Hampdens suffered heavy loses on their initial daylight raids and were soon withdrawn from service. Later, with improved defensive firepower and armour, they were used by Bomber Command in night raids with some success until September 1942.

First squadron to be equipped was No 49 at Scampton, which had received its full complement of aircraft by the end of November 1938. By the end of the year, Nos 50 and 83 Squadrons were re-equipping, and at the outbreak of war, Bomber Command could muster eight squadrons. When production ended, in 1942, a grand total of 1,530 Hampdens had been built, this figure including a number of Herefords which never became operational, many being converted to Hampdens.

Below: 'Flying Panhandle' over Radlett in April 1939; and (left) 'somewhere in England' a Hampden is loaded with parachute bombs. Symbols on the nose indicate that this aircraft has completed thirteen sorties.

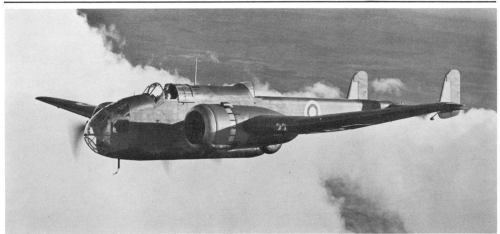

North American Harvard

The North American Harvard two-seat advanced trainer was one of the first American aircraft ordered for the RAF, in June 1938, and first equipped No 3 Flying Training School at Grantham in December of that year. Initial deliveries were of the Harvard I, equivalent to the US Army Air Corps' BC-1, some 200 being completed by June 1939. Later aircraft were characterised by their triangular fin and rudder and squared-off wing tips. Perhaps the most recognisable characteristic of this excellent trainer was the penetrating rasping note of its engine, caused by the propeller tips exceeding the speed of sound.

By the end of the war the main Harvard variant in service with Flying Training Command was the Mk IIB, powered by the 550-hp Pratt and Whitney Wasp R-1340-49 which gave it a top speed of 205 mph at 5,000 ft and a cruising speed of 170 mph.

1939-1948

Miles Master

The Miles Master was a two-seat advanced trainer powered by either a Rolls-Royce Kestrel XXX (Mk I), Bristol Mercury XX (Mk II), or Pratt and Whitney Wasp Junior (Mk III). Derived from the private venture Miles Kestrel, the prototype Master first flew in 1938. Production of the Mk I amounted to 900, the first being delivered to the RAF in mid-1939 for use by the Flying Training Schools at Sealand, Montrose and Hullavington.

The Master II first flew in November 1939 and the Mk III, shown here, the following year. Master IIs and IIIs were used primarily by No 5 (Pilot) Advanced Flying Unit at Ternhill from 1942. Total production of the Master had reached 3,450 when, in 1942, manufacture was ceased in order to make room on the production line for the Martinet high-speed target tug.

de Havilland Dominie

The twin-engined de Havilland Dominie was a militarized version of the Dragon Rapide and was used as a radio or navigation trainer or ten-seat communications aircraft, the former externally identifiable by the roof-mounted D/F loop aerial. Deliveries started in September 1939, and total production reached 521 (including some for the Fleet Air Arm), the majority of which were built by Brush Coachworks at Loughborough between 1943 and 1945.

This D.H.89 Dominie was purchased for Air Council use and was photographed in March 1935.

Bristol Blenheim IV

The Blenheim IV superseded the Mk I in production in late 1938 and differed from the earlier aircraft in only two major respects: a new forward fuselage with lengthened nose was fitted, and long-range tanks installed in the wings. In fact the first Mk IVs were converted Mk I airframes and did not have the long-range wings and were usually referred to as the Type 142S, later machines being designated Type 142L. Other improvements made during the war included armour plate, fitting of a free-mounted Vickers 'K' in the nose and a rearward firing .303-in Browning in a blister attached to the floor of the nose.

The first bomber squadron to be equipped with the new aircraft was No 90, in March 1939, and by the outbreak of war, Bomber Command had six squadrons of Blenheim IVs, forming No 2 Group. The Blenheim IV also flew operationally with Army Co-operation squadrons, with Coastal Command and, as the Mk IVF, with thirteen fighter squadrons.

Powered by two 920-hp Bristol Mercury XV engines, the Blenheim IV had a top speed of 266 mph at 11,800 ft and an endurance of more than eight and a half hours.

The Mk IV (left) was photographed in February 1939, while the Blenheim IVL (below) being bombed-up at Wattisham is from No 110 Squadron, photographed in September 1939.

Lockheed Hudson

The Lockheed Hudson I was the first American-built aircraft to see operational service with the RAF in the Second World War, equipping No 224 Squadron, Coastal Command, at Gosport in the summer of 1939. Initial deliveries were by sea, the first aircraft reaching Liverpool in February 1939; from November 1940, however, Hudsons were flown direct to Britain from Gander, Newfoundland, the Atlantic crossing to Aldergrove, Northern Ireland, taking 10½ hours.

The versatile Hudson served with several commands during the war. A Hudson I of No 224 Squadron claimed the first enemy aircraft shot down by an RAF aircraft in the Second World War: a Dornier Do 18 flying boat over Jutland, on October 8, 1939, and in one of the more bizarre actions of the war a Hudson III from No 269 Squadron accepted the surrender of *U-570* in the North Atlantic, in August 1941. Hudsons were also used for making secret landings in France to collect or deliver agents and supplies for the Resistance.

More than 800 Hudsons were delivered against British contracts before the first Hudson IIIAs began arriving under the lend-lease arrangement with America. Powered by two 1,100-hp Wright Cyclone GR-1820-G102A engines, the Hudson I had a maximum speed of 246 mph at 6,500 ft and an endurance of six hours.

These Hudsons are in the United States awaiting ferry pilots to bring them across the Atlantic. All aircraft over-flying US territory carried the white star insignia before their delivery into Allied hands.

Bristol Beaufort

The Bristol Beaufort torpedo bomber was a development of the Blenheim and superseded Coastal Command's obsolete Vickers Vildebeests from the end of 1939, the first aircraft going to No 22 Squadron based at Thorney Island. Total production of the Bristol Taurus VI-engined Beaufort was 1,013. This version had a top speed of 265 mph at 6,000 ft. The Beaufort was later re-engined with the American Pratt & Whitney Twin Wasp and a total of 415 was built, later aircraft of this Mark being built as trainers with the dorsal turret removed.

Standard shore-based British torpedo bomber during the first four years of the Second World War, the Beaufort was also used on maritime reconnaissance duties and as a minelayer. It was gradually replaced by the faster and much more agile Beaufighter TF.10 in the torpedo-strike role, and the last Beaufort was taken out of squadron service late in 1944.

Below is a Twin Wasp-engined Beaufort, photographed in August 1941. The two Beaufort Is (above), also photographed in 1941, are from No 42 Squadron, Coastal Command.

Boulton Paul Defiant

The Boulton Paul Defiant was initially built as the P.82 under the direction of J.D. North to meet Air Ministry specification F.9/35, issued in April 1935, calling for a two-seat fighter with all its armament concentrated in a single power-operated turret. At the time, great importance was attached by the Air Staff to this requirement and there were three other contenders, from Hawker, Bristol and Armstrong Whitworth. In the event, only the Hawker Hotspur and the Boulton Paul P.82 were selected for development, but the Hotspur did not go into production.

The first production Defiant Mk I flew in July 1939 and deliveries to No 264 Squadron began in December of that year. Hydraulic problems delayed the aircraft's operational debut until May 1940, but early engagements appeared to vindicate the concept of the turret fighter. The Luftwaffe, however, quickly appreciated the lack of forward armament and Defiant losses mounted so rapidly that the type was withdrawn from daylight operations in August of that year.

Later equipped with Airborne Interception (AI) radar, however, the Defiant proved to be a most useful night-fighter and was credited with the biggest number of kills per interception of any night-fighter type during the winter of 1940-41.

Powered by the 1,260-hp Rolls-Royce Merlin XX, the Defiant Mk II had a top speed of 315 mph at 16,400 ft. Total production of the Defiant ran to more than 1,000, and in addition to its night-fighter role, the Defiant was also used, in limited quantities, as a target tug and for air-sea rescue duties.

Top: Defiant I of No 410 Squadron, January 1942. Above: Defiant Is of No 264 Squadron, Kirton-in-Lindsay, August 1940.

Blackburn Botha

Designed to Air Ministry specification M.15/35, the Blackburn Botha was intended for either general reconnaissance or torpedo bombing and was a contemporary of the Beaufort and Saro Lerwick flying-boat. The first production Botha flew in July 1939 and deliveries began to No 608 (Coastal Command) Squadron in May 1940, replacing the squadron's Ansons.

The Botha was not a success, however, being seriously underpowered among other shortcomings, and the type was withdrawn from operational flying in November 1940, thereafter being used for operational training. It was declared obsolete in August 1943, although a few remained in service until September 1944.

Powered by two 880-hp Bristol Perseus X or 930-hp Bristol Perseus XA engines, the Botha had a top speed of 209 mph at sea level. Armament was one fixed forward-firing .303-in machine gun and two .303-in machine guns in a power-operated dorsal turret; a single torpedo could be carried internally.

Left: this Botha is from No 3 School of General Reconnaissance, Squire's Gate, Blackpool, and was photographed in September 1941. Botha I, L6468 (below), is from the same production batch.

Short Stirling

The Stirling has an important place in RAF history, being the first of the four-engined heavy bombers to enter service. Designed to Air Ministry specification B.12/36 of July 1936, the Stirling was from the outset intended as a four-engined aircraft, unlike the Halifax and Lancaster which both stemmed from twin-engined designs. Unfortunately, the specification included a limitation on wing span, so that the aircraft could be accommodated in a standard RAF hangar, and this resulted in a wing of low aspect ratio and a consequently adverse performance at altitude. A further limitation was imposed by the design of the Stirling's bomb-bay, which was divided into sections and thus restricted the maximum size of bomb which could be carried to 4,000 lb

The full-scale prototype was preceded by a half-scale aerodynamic prototype powered by four 90-hp Pobjoy Niagra radial engines, which first flew in September 1938. The full-scale prototype made its first flight in May 1939. Deliveries of the Stirling I commenced in August 1940, first equipping No 7 Squadron at Leeming.

By mid-1943 it was judged to be outmoded as a heavy bomber and was increasingly allotted the less well-defended targets. During its career with Bomber Command, it served with Nos 7, 15, 75, 90, 149, 196, 199, 214, 218, 622 and 623 Squadrons, as well as with No 138 and 624 (Special Duties) Squadrons. Apart from bombing, the Stirling was also used for minelaying and ECM duties, but from the beginning of 1944 its primary role was as a glider tug and transport, this variant being the Stirling IV. Total Stirling production, Mk I to IV, amounted to 2,221.

Above: Stirling I photographed in March 1942. 'G' for George, being bombed-up at Oakington, is from No 7 Squadron.

Bristol Beaufighter

The Bristol Beaufighter two-seat night-fighter or anti-shipping strike fighter was evolved from the original Bristol solution to the radical Air Ministry specification F.11/37, which called for a fighter with a heavily armed cannon turret. Leslie Frise and engine designer Roy Fedden proposed a private venture aircraft using the wings, tail unit and undercarriage of the Beaufort torpedo bomber combined with a new compact fuselage accommodating a crew of two, and using the more powerful Bristol Hercules sleeve-valve engines.

The Type 156 Beaufighter prototype was completed and almost ready to fly when an enthusiastic Air Ministry decided to adopt this aircraft in July 1939. Service evaluation trials began in April 1940, but the performance of fully armed aircraft fell below expectations, although installation of the more powerful Hercules XI in production Beaufighter IFs produced better results. The aircraft was also found to be prone to swing on take-off and to be longitudinally unstable at lower speeds.

Deliveries to the RAF began in late July 1940 and the first Beaufighters entered squadron service, with Nos 25, 29, 219 and 604 Squadrons, from September of that year. Equipped with the new AI Mk IV radar and armed with four 20-mm Hispano cannon mounted in the lower part of the fuselage nose and six .303-in Browning machine guns in the wings, the Beaufighter was a fearsome prospect for German raiders.

The Beaufighter was to see action on almost all fronts, operating in the Western Desert as a long-range day fighter, and from March 1941 Beaufighters began to replace Blenheim IVFs in Coastal Command fighter squadrons. The initial Coastal Command version was the Mk IC, and with the introduction of the torpedo-carrying Mk VC the type's versatility was further extended.

More than 5,500 Beaufighters of all Marks entered service with the RAF, the last serving aircraft being with No 45 Squadron in the Far East. During its career, it served with Nos 25, 27, 29, 46, 68, 89, 108, 125, 141, 153, 176, 177, 219, 255, 256, 307, 406, 409, 410, 456, 488, 515, 600 and 604 Fighter Squadrons.

SR914 is a Beaufighter TT.10 target-training aircraft from RAE Farnborough, photographed in July 1955.

Handley Page Halifax

The Handley Page Halifax followed the RAF's first four-engined bomber, the Short Stirling, into service by about three months, and together with Lancaster it was to share the major burden of Bomber Command's strategic night offensive against Germany. The Halifax was to be more than a heavy bomber, however, serving as paratroop transport and glider tug, long-range transport and maritime reconnaissance aircraft.

Initially designed as a medium-heavy bomber with two Rolls-Royce Vulture engines to specification B.13/36, it emerged in 1937 as a four Merlin-engined aircraft designated the Handley Page HP.57. The first unarmed prototype flew in October 1939 and the first production aircraft almost exactly one year later, powered by four 1,280-hp Merlin X engines giving it a top speed of 265 mph. Halifaxes first equipped No 35 Squadron operating from Linton-on-Ouse, their first operational sortie being a raid on Le Havre on the night of March 11-12 1941.

In all, some 6,176 Halifaxes were built for the RAF, serving with some thirty-four bomber squadrons, the last leaving Handley Page's Cricklewood factory on November 20, 1946. Seen here is a Halifax Mk II Series I.

Avro Manchester

The Avro Manchester was one of the great disappointments of the Second World War. Designed by Roy Chadwick as a twin-engined medium-heavy bomber to Air Ministry specification B.13/36, it soon became apparent that its operational failures were the result of underpowered and unreliable engines married to an otherwise excellent airframe.

The Manchester first entered service with No 207 Squadron at Waddington in November 1940 and their first operational use was on a raid against Brest on the night of 24-25 February 1941. The unorthodox Rolls-Royce Vulture engines failed frequently and the type was withdrawn from operational use in June 1942. The parent company built only 159 Manchesters, including the prototypes, and Metropolitan-Vickers built a further forty-three after losing the first thirteen when their works were bombed in December 1940. Maximum speed was 265 mph at 17,000 ft and maximum load was 10,350 lb.

Manchester Mk I coded EM-S, from No 207 Squadron, was photographed in November 1941, at which time the squadron was moving from Waddington to Bottesford. Below is the second prototype Manchester.

Westland Whirlwind

Notable as the first single-seat twin-engined fighter to see service with the RAF, the Westland Whirlwind was designed by W.E. Petter to the requirements of Air Ministry specification F.37/35. Highly manoeuvrable and with handling characteristics frequently described as delightful, the Whirlwind nevertheless suffered from that familiar problem of many new RAF aircraft of the time: engine teething troubles, with its 885-hp Rolls-Royce Peregrines. There were also difficulties with maintenance and operation from short grass fields was limited by the aircraft's high landing speed.

Deliveries began to No 263 Squadron at Exeter in July 1940, but the squadron suffered a number of casualties as a result of accidents. In the easy part of its operational life the Whirlwind served as a long-range escort fighter for light day bombers, but later in the war made a name for itself as a low-level fighter-bomber, attacking channel shipping, locomotives, bridges and harbour installations alongside the Hurri-bomber.

A second Whirlwind squadron, No 137, was formed in September 1941, but the type was withdrawn from service in 1943 after a total of 112 had been built. Armed with four fixed 20-mm Hispano cannon in the nose, the Whirlwind had a maximum speed of 315 mph at 5,000 ft.

Brewster Buffalo

Originally designed for the US Navy as a shipboard fighter, the Brewster Buffalo was chosen as a land fighter for the RAF by the British Purchasing Mission in 1939, a contract for 170 subsequently being placed. Following trials by No 71 Squadron at Church Fenton, the type was rejected as a first-line fighter in Europe and it was decided instead to divert the type to the Far East, where it was to be disastrously outclassed by Japanese Zeros.

No 67 Squadron in Singapore received its first Buffalos in March 1941, becoming fully operational in June of that year. After the fall of Singapore, however, in February 1942, surviving Buffalos co-operated with the American Volunteer Group in the defence of Burma.

Consolidated Catalina

The Catalina came to the attention of the Air Ministry in the late 1930s, and one example was flown to Britain for evaluation in July 1939 and delivered to the Marine Aircraft Experimental Establishment at Felixstowe. With the outbreak of war an initial order for thirty aircraft was placed, for Coastal Com-

mand, and the first of these, designated Catalina I, entered service in early 1941 with squadrons in Northern Ireland. An aircraft from No 209 Squadron, based at Castle Archdale, spotted the German battleship *Bismark* on May 26, 1941, after naval forces had lost contact.

The type subsequently operated

in the Indian Ocean, from Gibraltar during the North African landings in 1942 and even for a time from a base near Murmansk.

British Catalinas were armed with a single .303-in Vickers machine gun in the bow, twin Vickers guns in each of the beam blisters and a sixth Vickers firing

through a tunnel aft of the hull step. Bomb load was 2,000 lb and maximum speed of the Catalina IB was 190 mph at 10,500 ft on its two 1,200-hp Pratt & Whitney Twin Wasp R-1830-S1C3-G engines. Endurance was a creditable 17½ hours.

Vickers Wellington

The Vickers Wellington was Britain's most formidable bomber by the outbreak of war and formed the backbone of Bomber Command's night raids over Germany in the early years of the war before the four-engined bombers took over this task in large numbers. Known to one and all as the 'Wimpey', the Wellington was immensely strong, by virtue of its geodetic construction, and could absorb a great deal of flak damage.

First Wellington Is reached No 9 Squadron in October 1938 and by the time war commenced Bomber Command had six squadrons operational on the type. The main version with Bomber Command in 1941-42, however, was the Wellington III. This aircraft was powered by two 1,375-hp Bristol Hercules III or 1,500-hp Hercules XI engines and had a top speed of 255 mph at 12,500 ft. Defensive armament was a pair of .303-in machine guns in the nose, four .303s in the tail turret and two manually-operated .303 guns in the beam positions. Maximum bomb load was 4,500 lb.

In addition to its primary role as night bomber, the Wellington also gave valuable service to Coastal Command on maritime reconnaissance duties and was also used by Transport Command. The final bomber variant was the Wellington B Mk X, powered by a pair of Bristol Hercules VI or XVI engines. An improved version of the Mk III, it served widely with Bomber Command, the Middle East Air Forces and Operational Training Units. Total production of Wellingtons of all Marks was 11,461, the last of which was delivered in October 1945. During its career with Bomber Command, the Wellington served with a total of forty-six front-line squadrons.

Curtiss Tomahawk

The Curtiss Tomahawk was developed from the earlier radial-engined Mohawk and was used by the RAF as a single-seat tactical reconnaissance and ground-attack fighter. In RAF service the Tomahawk I corresponded to the USAAF's P-40A, the IIA to the P-40B and the Tomahawk IIB to the P-40C. Total deliveries to the RAF of all three versions was 885 aircraft, the first of which entered service with No 2 Squadron in Britain in August 1941. Overseas, the first Desert Air Force squadron to be fully equipped with Tomahawks was No 112 Squadron, which replaced its Gladiators in June 1941.

Powered by a 1,040-hp Allison V-1710-33 twelve cylinder liquid-cooled engine, the Tomahawk IIB was capable of a top speed of 345 mph at 15,000 ft. Armament was six .303-in machine guns, two in the fuselage and four mounted in the wings.

AH762 is a Tomahawk I, photographed at Bath in February 1941. The flight of three aircraft are Tomahawk IIBs, photographed in April 1942.

Douglas Havoc

The Douglas Havoc was a night-fighter and night-intruder version of the Boston light bomber and was produced in an effort to fill the serious shortage of RAF aircraft capable of carrying the cumbersome and heavy early airborne interception radar. Modification of ex-French DB-7 bombers took place at the Burtonwood Aircraft Repair depot during the winter of 1940-41. Armour protection for the crew of three was provided, flame-damping exhausts fitted and four forward-firing .303-in Browning machine guns installed in the lower part of the fuselage nose, with a single Vickers 'K' in the rear cockpit. These aircraft were originally known as Rangers and first equipped No 23 Squadron at Ford on intrusion duties.

For night-fighting purposes, the Havoc I was fitted with a 'solid' nose housing AI Mk IV radar and eight .303-in machine guns. The type first became operational with No 85 Squadron in April 1941. The Havoc I Turbinlite was a modification of thirty-one aircraft which had the 2,700 million candlepower Helmore/GEC searchlight installed in addition to AI radar to illuminate enemy bombers for the benefit of accompanying night-fighters.

The Havoc II, also produced as a Turbinlite aircraft, had the Wright Double Cyclone engines and was fitted with a new nose housing a phenomenal twelve .303-in Brownings. Maximum speed of the Twin Wasp-engined Havoc I was 295 mph at 13,000 ft

Airborne from Ford is this Havoc I intruder of No 23 Squadron, photographed in the summer of 1941. Havoc II, AH552, (far right) is fitted with the 'bow-and-arrow' AI radar aerial.

Douglas Boston

The Douglas Boston III was the first of the American DB-7 series of aircraft to be used by the RAF in its designed light-bomber role, first entering service with No 88 Squadron at Swanton Morley in October 1941, replacing Blenheim IVs. They were used by No 2 Group on anti-shipping strikes and daylight raids on Continental fringe targets. From November 1942, the Boston III had entered service in North Africa, and in August 1943 home-based Bostons began operations with the newly-formed 2nd Tactical Air Force.

The Boston IV, equipped with a power-operated dorsal turret, began operations with the RAF from the summer of 1944, and some 256 Mks IV and V were allocated to Britain via Lend-Lease. Powered by two 1,600-hp Wright Double Cyclone radial engines, the Boston III had a top speed of 204 mph at 13,000 ft and had a range of 1,020 miles with its maximum bomb load of 2,000 lb. Seen here are Boston IIIs of No 107 Squadron, based at Great Massingham, Norfolk, photographed in November 1942.

Supermarine Spitfire V

First deliveries to Fighter Command of the Spitfire V began in February 1941, to No 92 Squadron. Three sub-variants of the Mk V were produced: the VA with eight .303-in Browning machine guns in the wings, the VB with two 20-mm cannon and four .303-in machine guns, and the VC which introduced a 'universal wing' capable of taking either the A or B armament or four 20-mm cannon. Powered by the 1,440-hp Rolls-Royce Merlin 45,

the Spitfire V had a maximum speed of 374 mph at 13,000 ft, or 357 mph at 6,000 ft with clipped wings. In addition to its gun armament, the Mk V had provision for a centre-line mounted 500-lb bomb, or two wing-mounted 250-lb bombs and was the first version to be used as a fighter-bomber and the first to be used overseas. For tropical duties an air filter was fitted beneath the nose. A total of 6,464 Mk Vs was built, and from 1943

most of these had clipped wings for improved low-altitude manoeuvrability.

Development of the Spitfire was rapid and was largely geared to increases in engine power. To combat the superior Focke-Wulf Fw190, the Spitfire IX was produced as a stop-gap before the arrival of the Mk VII. In the event the Mk IX became the more widely used, with its 1,660-hp Merlin 61 fitted with two-speed, two-stage

supercharger, and a total of 5,739 was built. First squadron to be equipped was No 64 Squadron at Hornchurch, in July 1942. Fitted with the 'universal' wing, it had a top speed of 408 mph at 25,000 ft.

Flying in echelon starboard are three Spitfire VBs from No 243 Squadron, based at Ouston in the summer of 1942.

Supermarine Walrus

The Supermarine Walrus was a development of the private venture Seagull V which first flew in June 1933. Known universally and affectionately as the 'Shagbat' the Walrus II came into its own as an air-sea rescue aircraft. One of the pioneer units engaged in those duties was No 276 Squadron, based at Bircham Newton, which operated the Walrus, Lysander and Anson on rescue work from late 1941.

Most of the ASR aircraft were Walrus Mk IIs with a wooden hull and deployment of these largely Saro-built aircraft was with seven home-based ASR squadrons, four Middle East ASR squadrons and one mine-spotting unit. Fitted with a 775-hp Bristol Pegasus VI engine, the Walrus II had a top speed of 135 mph and cruised at 95 mph.

Hawker Typhoon

Originally projected in 1937 by Sydney Camm as a future Hurricane replacement, the Hawker Typhoon was developed in parallel with the Vulture-engined Tornado to specification F.18/37. The Tornado programme was abandoned in early 1941 with the withdrawal of the unsuccessful Vulture engine, and the Sabre-engined Typhoon was lucky not to go the same way, early flight tests indicating several undesirable handling qualities, together with a clutch of problems from the under-developed engine.

The first production Typhoon IA, with the 2,200-hp Napier Sabre IIA engine, was flown in late May 1941 and was armed with twelve wing-mounted .303-in Browning machine guns. The Typhoon IB, which followed close on the heels of the IA, was armed with four wing-mounted 20-mm Hispano cannon. The first units to receive the new aircraft were Nos 56 and 609 Squadrons at Duxford in September 1941 and it was soon found that the Typhoon was not only unsuccessful as an interceptor but also prone to discard its tail assembly during high-speed manoeuvres and many more Typhoons were lost through accidents than through enemy action.

By the end of 1942, however, with the rectification of the structural problems and the progressive solution of the Sabre's troubles, the Typhoon was increasingly used for offensive operations, carrying two 250-lb bombs beneath its wings. Aircraft from Nos 174, 181, 245 and 609 Squadrons enjoyed considerable success in their sweeps across France, Belgium and Holland and before long Typhoons had become famous for their train-busting activities, with as many as 150 locomotives being destroyed each month. With the Typhoon's modification to carry rocket projectiles the aircraft finally came into its element and its destruction of German radar stations along the channel coast helped enormously in maintaining the tactical surprise of the Allied landings in Normandy in June 1944.

Above left: Typhoon Mk1A on armament trials at Boscombe Down. Centre, a Typhoon IB from No 183 Squadron, and below it a two-gun Typhoon FR. IB.

Curtiss Kittyhawk

The Curtiss Kittyhawk single-seat fighter-bomber was the last of the American Curtiss P-40 series to be used by the RAF and the type served exclusively with the Middle East Air Forces in the Western Desert and, later, in Sicily and Italy. A development of the Tomahawk, the Kittyhawk I differed chiefly in having a more powerful Allison engine in a modified cowling, a re-designed cockpit canopy and revised armament. The Kittyhawk IA, equivalent to the USAAF's P-40E, had six wing-mounted .5-in machine guns.

Used primarily at low altitudes and for close support, the Kittyhawk was effective in disrupting Rommel's Panzer forces with its maximum bomb load of 1,000 lb, usually comprised of one 500-lb beneath the fuselage and two 250-lb bombs below the wings. Maximum speed was 362 mph at 5,000 ft on its 1,600-hp Allison engine.

Martin Baltimore

The Martin Baltimore was used by the RAF exclusively in the Mediterranean theatre and, unlike the earlier Maryland reconnaissance bomber which had been absorbed from French contracts, was built specifically to British require-ments. A four-seat light bomber, it was powered by a pair of 1,660-hp Wright Double Cyclone engines which gave it a top speed of 302 mph at 11,000 ft. Maximum bomb load was 2,000 lb.

Introduced in January 1942, the early aircraft were Mk I and Mk II types without the power-operated dorsal turret. Appearance of the Baltimore III introduced the Boulton Paul twin-gun turret, but this was substituted on the Mk IV and Mk V aircraft by the Martin dorsal turret. Operated both by night and by day, the Baltimores were used to excellent effect in Tunisia, Sicily and later in Italy ahead of the advancing armies.

Hawker Hurricane IIC

The Hawker Hurricane IIC was the first Mark of that illustrious aircraft to be armed with four wing-mounted cannon, and it could also carry two 250-lb or 500-lb bombs beneath the wings. First home-based squadrons to receive Mk IICs were Nos 1 and 3 in 1941, but by 1942 the Hurricane was outmoded as an interceptor fighter. However, it continued to serve with distinction in the Western Desert and in the Far East as a night-fighter.

In North Africa, the 'tank-buster' Hurricane IID, carrying two Vickers Type S 40-mm cannon, first saw action in early June 1942 with No 6 Squadron. Maximum speed was 290 mph at 12,000 ft.

Left: this Hurricane IIC, from No 34 Squadron, is fitted with a pair of 90-gallon ferry tanks. Below: Hurricane IV, KZ193, with tropical air filter and twin 40-mm Vickers guns. This aircraft is one of two later experimentally converted to Hurricane V configuration, with the installation of a ground-boosted Merlin 32 driving a Rotol four-bladed propeller. After protracted trials at Langley and Service Evaluation at Boscome Down both aircraft were returned to Hawker Aircraft for re-conversion to Mk IV standard.

Avro Lancaster

The Avro Lancaster was without doubt the most successful of Bomber Command's heavy bombers during the Second World War, and one of the most famous aircraft of all time. Ironically, the Lancaster came about because of the failure of its twin-engined predecessor, the Manchester. In fact the prototype Lancaster was known as the Manchester III and was a converted Manchester airframe with longer-span wings accommodating four Rolls-Royce Merlin engines and even retained the third central fin.

The first production Lancaster I flew for the first time in October 1941 and differed from the prototypes in having the more powerful 1,280-hp Merlin XX engines in place of the Merlin Xs; as production progressed the engines were changed for Merlin 22s and later for the 1,620-hp Merlin 24s.

The Lancaster I first equipped No 44 Squadron at Waddington in early 1942, followed by No 97 Squadron at Woodhall Spa. In order to maintain the flow of Lancaster to squadrons in the event of a break in the supply of Merlin engines a Bristol Hercules VI-powered version, the Lancaster II, was put into production at Armstrong Whitworth's Bagington factory, but only 300 of this version were built.

The Lancaster contained enormous growth potential, particularly in relation to the size of its bomb-load. In April 1942, for instance, Lancasters dropped the first 8,000-lb bombs, and in June 1944 the first deep-penetration 12,000-lb Tallboy bombs were dropped. Largest of all were the 22,000-lb Grand Slam or Earthquake bombs dropped on the Bielefeld Viaduct in March 1945. During the war, Lancasters dropped a total of 600,000 tons of bombs and more than 7,300 Lancasters were built, including a number in Canada by Victory Aircraft. The type continued to fly post-war as photo-reconnaissance, maritime-reconnaissance and air-sea rescue aircraft.

Below: this Avro Lancaster Mk I, photographed in mid-1942, was from No 50 Squadron. DS778 (right) was one of only three hundred Lancaster Mk IIs built.

de Havilland Mosquito B.IV

The de Havilland Mosquito was an outstandingly successful design and was operated during the war (and in some versions long afterwards) as a reconnaissance aircraft, light bomber and night-fighter. The company's experience in the design and construction of high-performance wooden aircraft convinced them that it was quite possible to build a bomber without defensive armament which would outfly all contemporary fighters. The original twin Merlin-engined private venture design was turned down by the Air Ministry in 1938, but with the outbreak of war, and thanks largely to Sir Wilfrid Freeman, Air Council Member for Research, Development and Production, de Havillands were sanctioned to commence detailed design work on a light bomber having a range of 1,500 miles and carrying a bomb load of 1,000 lb.

Designated D.H.98 Mosquito, the prototype flew for the first time at Hatfield on November 25, 1940, less than eleven months from the start of design work. Like so many aircraft that look right the Mosquito flew right, and the performance surprised even the manufacturers who discovered that they had built the world's fastest operational aircraft.

By July 1941, large-scale production of the first bomber variant, the B.IV, was underway and the type first entered service with No 2 (Light Bomber) Group, equipping No 105 Squadron at Swanton Morley in November that year. The first operational sortie was made on May 31, 1942, when four of No 105 Squadron's B.IVs made a daylight raid on Cologne.

The final bomber variant was the B.35, the prototype of which flew in March 1945. By this time the aircraft's performance and load carrying capacity had increased almost out of recognition, maximum speed having risen to 415 mph, ceiling to 42,000ft and, like its predecessor the B.XVI, it could carry a 4,000-lb 'cookie' in its bulged bomb-bay. However, it was just too late to see operational service.

Mosquito bombers were finally superseded in Bomber Command by the first Canberras in 1952-53.

These two Mosquito B.IVs, from No 105 Squadron, were photographed in December 1942. At the time, the squadron was based at Marham.

North American Mustang

The North American Mustang I was designed from the outset to British requirements following a visit by the British Purchasing Mission, and the prototype was built in the unprecedented time of 117 days from the start of design in April 1940. First flight was in October 1940, and the Mustang's performance was found to be superior to contemporary American fighters at all but higher altitudes, where engine power fell away.

The first aircraft reached Britain in October 1941 and because of its lack of performance at altitude it was decided to employ it in the armed tactical reconnaissance role, rather than as an interceptor fighter. First deliveries were to No 2 Squadron at Sawbridgeworth in April 1942, where the Mustang supplanted the Army Co-operation Tomahawks.

The later Merlin-engined Mustang Mks III and IV, however, became widely used as long-range escort fighters and fighter-bombers. The first Mustang IIIs equipped No 19 Squadron at Ford in February 1944 and later crossed to France with the 2nd Tactical Air Force.

More than 2,600 Mustangs of all versions served with the RAF and some were retained by Fighter Command as late as November 1946. Powered by a 1,680-hp Packard Merlin V-1650-7, the Mustang III had a maximum speed of 442 mph at 24,500 ft, was armed with four .50-calibre machine guns and could carry up to 1,000 lb of bombs.

The top photograph shows Mustang I, AG357, experimentally fitted with rocket projectiles, while below it is the Merlin-engined Mustang III prototype, photographed in October 1942.

Consolidated Liberator

The Liberator was used by the RAF as either a general reconnaissance and anti-submarine aircraft, heavy bomber or unarmed transport aircraft.

It was used in comparatively large numbers by Coastal Command, first equipping No 120 Squadron, and did much to help in the battle against the U-boats operating in the Atlantic because of its exceptional range. The Liberator II was the first variant to be equipped with power-operated gun turrets and as well as joining the Liberator Is of No 120 Squadron was used by Nos 59 and 86 Squadrons on long-range anti-submarine duties. Overseas, the Liberator was used as a heavy bomber, in the Middle East and later in India.

The Liberator IIIA was the first of the the Lend-Lease variants, and Coastal Command went on to operate the G.R.V, G.R.VI and finally the G.R.VIII.

This Liberator G.R.V was an experimental aircraft with chin ASV, earlier wing and fuselage ASV, and rocket projectile sponsons. The Leigh light is under the starboard wing.

Douglas Dakota

The Douglas Dakota was a development of the DC-3 commercial airliner of the mid-1930s and formed the mainstay of RAF and USAAF transport squadrons during the war, serving in every battle zone. Supplied under Lend-Lease, the RAF received more than 1,900 of the type, the first of which were supplied to No 31 Squadron in Burma in June 1942, where they replaced DC-2s and Valentias.

More than twenty-five wartime squadrons were equipped with various Marks of the Dakota, which was used as glider tug, paratroop carrier, personnel transport, freighter and air ambulance. After the war the Dakota continued to operate with the RAF and the Service's last 'Dak' was retired on April 1, 1970.

This one is about to snatch-launch a Waco Hadrian glider, at Farnborough in July 1950.

Lockheed Ventura

Bearing a superficial resemblence to the Hudson maritime reconnaissance aircraft, the Lockheed Ventura was a military development of the Lodestar transport and was used by the RAF initially in three Bomber Command squadrons as a light day-bomber, first entering service with No 21 Squadron in October 1942. It was not particularly successful on daylight raids and after being withdrawn from Bomber Command in 1943 it re-emerged in Coastal Command as a general reconnaissance aircraft and was chiefly used on meteorological flights.

Powered by two 2,000-hp Pratt & Whitney Double Wasp engines, the Ventura II had a maximum speed of 300 mph.

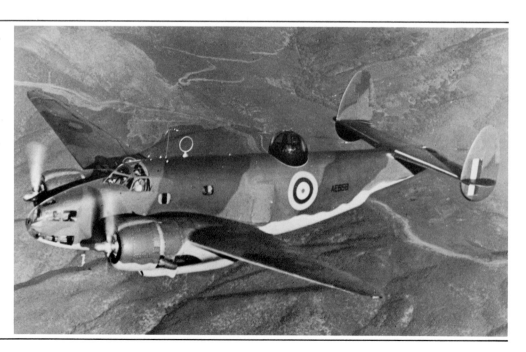

North American Mitchell

The North American Mitchell was known as the B-25 in USAAF service, first entering service in 1941. With the RAF, Mitchells were used mainly by No 2 Group squadrons as a light day-bomber, and more than 800 were delivered, the majority of which were Mitchell IIs, corresponding to the USAAF's B-25C. First deliveries were to Nos 98 and 180 Squadrons at West Raynham in September 1942. From August 1943 they operated with the 2nd Tactical Air Force, making pre-invasion attacks on targets in northern France.

Powered by two 1,350-hp Wright Double Cyclone engines, the Mitchell I had a top speed of 292 mph at 15,000 ft, cruising at 210 mph. Range was 1,635 miles with 4,000 lb of bombs, or 950 miles with the maximum load of 6,000 lb.

This Mitchell II of No 180 Squadron was photographed in April 1943.

Martin Marauder

The Martin Marauder was originally designed as a medium bomber for the USAAF with the designation B-26 and first operated in the Pacific theatre in early 1942. In RAF use the Marauder served exclusively in the Middle East, the first aircraft equipping No 14 Squadron in August 1942 as a replacement for the squadron's Blenheims. Despite the aircraft's reputation for being difficult to handle the squadron completed conversion training without trouble and the Marauder became one of the most successful and popular aircraft of the war.

The Marauder III first entered RAF service with No 39 Squadron at Campomarino, Southern Italy, in December 1944 and, like the Marauder II, was fitted with the new longer (72 ft) span wing which improved handling, especially at low speeds. These Marauders of the Desert Air Force were used in support of the Allied invasion of Italy.

Powered by two 2,000-hp Pratt & Whitney Double Wasp radial engines, the Marauder III was capable of a top speed of 305 mph at 15,000 ft and could carry a maximum bomb load of 4,000 lb.

Armstrong Whitworth Albemarle

Although the prototype Armstrong Whitworth Albemarle flew as early as March 1940, the type did not enter squadron service until the beginning of January 1943. The first thirty-two Albemarles were completed as bombers, to Air Ministry specification B.18/38, which called for the aircraft to be built from composite wood and steel materials in order to conserve precious light alloys. It was decided, however, to utilize the type as a glider tug and special transport with the airborne forces and the first thirty-two aircraft were accordingly modified.

The first Albemarles were supplied to No 295 Squadron in January 1943 and total production of the type eventually reached 600. As a glider tug the Albemarle was first used operationally in the invasion of Sicily in July 1943, with Nos 296 and 297 Squadrons.

Powered by two Bristol Hercules XI engines the Albemarle cruised at 170 mph, with a maximum speed of 265 mph at 20,500 ft.

Vultee Vengeance

The Vultee Vengeance two-seat dive-bomber was built in the USA to a British specification dated July 1940, raised as a result of the startling successes won by the German Ju 87 Stukas. By the time the aircraft arrived in Britain, however, it was apparent that the dive-bomber could only survive in conditions of local air superiority and the type was diverted to the Far East, where it began operations in Burma in July 1943.

Total deliveries to the RAF were 1,205 aircraft, consisting of Marks I, II and III (equivalent to the USAAF's A-31), and Mk IVs (equivalent to USAAF A-35s). Some of the later RAF Mk IVs were converted for target-towing duties and were used both at home and overseas, designated Vengeance TT.IV.

Powered by a 1,700-hp Wright Double Cyclone radial engine, the Vengeance I had a top speed of 279 mph and could carry up to 2,000 lb of bombs.

Supermarine Sea Otter

Designed to supersede the famous Walrus, the Supermarine Sea Otter was supplied to both the Fleet Air Arm and RAF, entering service with the latter in the air-sea rescue role at the end of 1943 as the Sea Otter II. Last biplane of any type to serve with the RAF, the Sea Otter was built by Saro and differed from the Walrus in having an 885-hp Bristol Mercury engine driving a tractor propeller and the type also had better aerodynamic and hydrodynamic qualities.

At home, Sea Otters operated from Coastal Command stations in the south of England, equipping Nos 276, 278, 281 and 292 Squadrons, while overseas they did much valuable service during the Burma campaign of 1944-45, equipping Nos 135, 1351 and 1252 Air/Sea Rescue Flights.

The prototype, seen leaving the slipway at Vickers, was fitted with a contra-rotating propeller.

Hawker Tempest V

The idea for the Tempest originated in 1941, as a suggested Typhoon improvement incorporating a thinner eliptical wing to stave off compressibility effects and the new Sabre EC.107C engine. The initial proposal submitted to Air Ministry specification F.10/41 was called the Typhoon II and two prototypes were ordered in November 1941. However, further changes had to be made, principally lengthening the fuselage to accommodate fuel tanks that could no longer be located in the new thinner wing, and the addition of a dorsal fin, and the name of the new fighter was changed to Tempest.

The first Tempest to fly was the prototype Mk V, in early September 1942, fitted with the Sabre II engine. This was followed in February 1943 by the Tempest I fitted with the Sabre IV and leading-edge radiators. Because of difficulties with the Sabre IV, attention – and production con-

tracts – was diverted to the Tempest V with its tried and trusted Napier Sabre II, and this was the only version to see war service, first equipping Nos 3 and 486 Squadrons in April 1944. Although it was involved in some ground straffing operations in Northern

France after the invasion, it was in its attacks against the German V-1 flying bombs that the Tempest is probably best remembered and is credited with the destruction of 638 out of the RAF's total of 1,771 V-1s between June 13 and September 5, 1944.

Powered by the 2,180-hp Napier Sabre II, the Tempest V had a maximum speed of 426 mph at 17,800 ft and was armed with four 20-mm Hispano cannon in the wings and had provision for rocket projectiles or 2,000 lb of bombs beneath the wings.

de Havilland Mosquito Fighter

Originally conceived as a high-speed light bomber, later used as an unarmed photo-reconnaissance aircraft, the de Havilland Mosquito's third spectaculary successful area of operations was either as a radar-equipped night-fighter or ground-attack fighter-bomber. Home-based Mosquito night-fighters are credited with the destruction of 600 enemy aircraft during the three years that they were responsible for the defence of wartime Britain.

The first fighter prototype to fly was in May 1941, fitted with the then highly secret AI Mk.IV radar. The first squadrons to be equipped with the new night-fighter were Nos 157 at Castle Camps, followed by No 23 at Ford, in January 1942. Constant improvements were made to the aircraft, mainly to the AI radar which swapped its 'bow-and-arrow' aerial for the nose-mounted dish with the introduction of the centimetric AI Mk VIII. The last night-fighter variant to see war service was the Mosquito NF.30 which was introduced in 1944, but the last night-fighter of all was the N.F.38, which first flew in November 1947.

Equally successful was the series of Mosquito fighter-bombers, the most widely used of which was the Mk VI which first flew in February 1943.

Republic Thunderbolt

During the Second World War the RAF operated the American-built Republic Thunderbolt in both of its major versions: the Thunderbolt I, equivalent to the USAAF's P-47B 'Razorback', and the Thunderbolt II, equivalent to the P-47D, fitted with the 'tear-drop' moulded canopy. Both versions were used exclusively in Burma as fighter-bombers, a total of 830 serving with no fewer than sixteen RAF squadrons.

Powered by a 2,300-hp Pratt & Whitney Double Wasp R-2800-59 engine, the Thunderbolt II had a maximum speed of 427 mph and was armed with eight .50-calibre guns, with provision for 2,000 lb of bombs.

This well-known photograph shows a section of Thunderbolt Is overflying the airfield at Ratnap at the end of 1944 while another aircraft from No 134 Squadron is serviced.

Vickers Warwick

Originally conceived as a replacement for the Wellington, the Vickers Warwick, which first flew in August 1939, was disappointing as a bomber primarily because of problems with the engines; consequently only sixteen were completed for that role, the other 845, being adapted for other roles.

In January 1943 it was decided to convert the Warwick for air-sea rescue duties, carrying an open lifeboat designed by Air Commodore Waring and Uffa Fox, or Lindholme life-saving gear. This version, the Warwick ASR.I, entered service with No 280 Squadron at Langham, Norfolk in the summer of 1943. Final version of the Warwick was the Centaurus-powered GR.Mk.V which first equipped No 179 Squadron at St Eval, Cornwall, in 1945. Too late to see war service, it served with Coastal Command for a short time after the war.

The Warwick III was a long-range transport version with capacity for twenty-four troops. Only 100 were built, serving with Nos 46 and 47 Groups, Transport Command, from early 1945 to 1946.

Powered by two 2,520-hp Bristol Centaurus VII engines, the Warwick GR.Mk.V was capable of a maximum speed of 290 mph and could carry up to 2,000 lb of bombs.

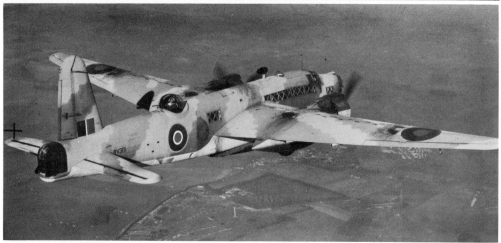

Gloster Meteor I

The Gloster Meteor I was not only the first jet aircraft to enter squadron service with the RAF, it was also the first and only Allied jet to see operational service during the Second World War. It was designed by Gloster Aircraft to specification F.9/40 and the twin-engined layout was adopted because of the low power of the available turbojets. An order for twelve prototypes was placed in February 1941 and the first aircraft flew in July 1943. The production order, placed in September 1941, called for twenty aircraft for which the name Thunderbolt was reserved, but this was changed to Meteor in March 1943, and the first production aircraft were delivered to the RAF in 1944, No 616 Squadron at Culmhead receiving its first two aircraft on July 12, 1944. By the end of August the squadron had converted entirely to Meteors and early in 1945 one flight was detached to join the 2nd TAF in Europe. The Meteors used in Europe were of the later Mk III type and were the first Meteors to be produced in quantity for the RAF.

The Mk III continued on the production line until superseded by the F.4 in 1945, although Meteor F.3s (as they were later to be designated) formed the equipment of Fighter Command's first post-war jet fighter wing, which comprised Nos 56, 74 and 245 Squadrons, stationed at Bentwaters, Suffolk. The F.3s were replaced in 1948 by the new F.4s which had the up-rated Derwent 5 engines. The F.4 was also used to equip the RAF's High-speed Flight and succeeded in setting up a new world's speed record on November 7, 1945 of 606 mph, at Herne Bay. The record was regained in September 1946 at Tangmere when Group Captain E.M. Donaldson achieved 616 mph.

Boeing Fortress

RAF bombing operations with the Boeing Fortress I, which it received in May 1941, were not particularly successful and surviving aircraft were transferred to Coastal Command in October 1942 for maritime reconnaissance duties. They were joined by the much improved Fortress II, British version of the B-17E, the first of which entered service with No 59 Squadron at Thorney Island in August 1942. About 200 Fortress II, IIA and III aircraft were delivered to the RAF, the Mks II and IIA joining Coastal Command's Liberators on Very Long Range (VLR) anti-submarine patrols.

The RAF's Fortress IIIs (equivalent to the USAAF's B-17G) incorporated the additional power-operated gun turret fitted beneath the nose and were used by Nos 214 and 223 Squadrons of No 100 Group on radio countermeasures duties from January 1944 to July 1945. Powered by four 1,200-hp Wright Cyclone GR-1820-97 engines, the Fortress III was capable of a maximum speed of 280 mph at 20,000 ft and had a range of 1,140 miles.

Avro Lincoln

Designed to specification B.14/43, the Avro Lincoln was intended to succeed the Lancaster in Bomber Command but was too late to see service in the Second World War. Nevertheless, it became the mainstay of post-war bomber squadrons in the RAF and a total of 528 was built.

The prototype first flew from Ringway on June 9, 1944 and the first Lincoln B.1s entered service with No 57 Squadron at East Kirby in August 1945 and were due to join Tiger Force for the bombing of Japan when that country surrendered. Lincolns did, however, see active service against the terrorists in Malaya and against the Mau Mau in Kenya. The last RAF aircraft, from RAF Signals Command, were withdrawn in March 1963.

Powered by four Rolls-Royce Merlin 85s, the Lincoln B.1 had a maximum speed of 295 mph at 15,000 ft and cruised at 215 mph at 20,000 ft. Range with its maximum bomb load of 14,000 lb was 1,470 miles.

Lincoln B.2, DX-F, from No 57 Squadron, Lindholme, photographed in September 1946 and below, a Lincoln B.2 refuelling a Meteor F.4.

Avro York

The Avro York long-range transport did not enter large-scale service with the RAF until after the war, primarily because, by agreement with the USA, the British aircraft industry during the war had concentrated on the design of fighters and bombers, leaving the transports to American manufacturers.

Designed to specification C.1/42, the prototype York used the same wings, undercarriage and engines as the Lancaster bomber but introduced a new, deeper fuselage. It first flew in July 1942 but the first squadron was not fully equipped until No 511 Squadron at Lyneham received its aircraft in 1945. By the time of the Berlin Air-

lift in 1948 the RAF had seven York squadrons, all of which were fully employed, making some 29,000 flights and carrying approximately 230,000 tons of supplies to the city. Yorks were eventually superseded in Transport Command by Handley Page Hastings aircraft.

Sikorsky Hoverfly

The Sikorsky Hoverfly I was the first type of helicopter to be used by the RAF and joined the Helicopter Training Flight at Andover early in 1945. The Hoverfly II arrived in Britain in 1946 and was used by both the Fleet Air Arm and RAF, a total of twenty-six being delivered. Powered by a 245-Franklin engine it could achieve a top speed of 100 mph and a had a service ceiling of 10,000 ft.

Shown here is a Hoverfly II photographed in August 1949.

Supermarine Spitfire F.21

The Griffon-engined Spitfire F.21, which first entered service in 1946, was more than 3,100 lb heavier than the Spitfire VC of 1941, some 80 mph faster in level flight and to look at them side-by-side it was nearly impossible to believe that they both came from the same stable. The F.21 was preceded by five other Griffon-engined versions, the first of which, the Mk XII, first entered service with Nos 41 and 91 Squadrons at Hawkinge in the Spring of 1943, powered by the 1,735-hp Griffon III or IV engine. The Spitfire XIV was the first with the two-stage 2,050-hp Griffon 65 driving a five-blade propeller, and featured a re-designed airframe with longer nose and broad fin and rudder. It first entered service with No 610 Squadron in January 1944 at West Malling.

Following the Spitfire XIV on the production line was the beefed up Mk XVIII, of which a total of 300 was built, comprising 100 fighter and 200 fighter-reconnaissance aircraft. Post-war, it served for a number of years with squadrons of the Middle and Far East Air Forces. After the XVIII came the final photo-reconnaissance version, the XIX, some 225 of which were supplied home and overseas. A PR.19 had the distinction of making the RAF's last operational Spitfire sortie, the flight being made by an aircraft from No 81 Squadron in Malaya, on April 1, 1954.

The Supermarine Spitfire F.21 was the first of the re-designed and re-engineered post-war aircraft and was followed by the F.22, which had a bubble canopy; some F.22s were fitted with 2,375-hp Griffon 65 and contra-rotating propeller. Final Spitfire variant was the F.24 with Spiteful-type tail assembly. Total Griffon-engined Spitfire production was 2,036 aircraft. Both aircraft shown here are F.22s.

de Havilland Vampire 1

The de Havilland Vampire was the second jet fighter to enter service with the RAF, but was too late to see active service during the Second World War, the first F.1s equipping No 247 Squadron in April 1946. Initially known as the Spider Crab, the Vampire was designed to specification E.6/41, the twin-boom layout being chosen to minimise the length of the jet-pipe and thus the power losses. The prototype first flew at Hatfield in September 1943, powered by a 2,700-lb thrust de Havilland Goblin turbojet.

The Vampire F.3 superseded the F.1 in Fighter Command, in Germany and with Auxiliary Air Force squadrons, some F.3s remaining with the AAF until as late as 1952. Six F.3s of No 54 Squadron were the first RAF jet aircraft to cross the Atlantic, in July 1948, staging through Iceland, Greenland and Labrador.

First of the fighter-bomber variants was the Vampire FB.5 which had cut-down wing-tips, strengthened skinning on the wings and a longer-stroke undercarriage to cope with the increased loaded weight resulting from the provision for 2,000 lb of underwing stores. It first flew in June 1948 and later

supplanted F.3s in remaining Fighter Command Vampire squadrons. The FB.9 was simply a tropicalised version of the FB.5 with an air-conditioned cockpit for service in the Far and Middle East.

Powered by a 3,300-lb thrust de Havilland Goblin 3, the FB.9 had a top speed of 548 mph at 30,000 ft and was armed with four 20-mm cannon.

This Vampire F.3 (above) was

photographed up from Hatfield in August 1947 and was one of a batch built by English Electric. Below it are Vampire Is of No 247 Squadron, based at Odiham between 1946 and 1948.

de Havilland Hornet

The single-seat de Havilland Hornet, like the jet-powered Vampire, was just too late to see action with the RAF in the Second World War, the first aircraft equipping No 64 Squadron at Horsham St Faith in May 1946. Designed as a long-range fighter or fighter-bomber, the Hornet was initiated as a private venture which was later to have specification F.12/43 written around it by an enthusiastic Air Ministry. The prototype first flew in July 1944 and proved to have beautiful handling characteristics and phenomenal performance, a repeat of the Mosquito's debut.

Powered by two 2,030-hp Rolls-Royce Merlins driving four-bladed propellers rotating in opposite directions, the Hornet F.3 had a maximum speed of 474 mph at 22,000 ft and was armed with four nose-mounted 20-mm cannon.

The Hornet remained in Fighter Command until replaced by Meteors, starting in 1951, and during its career saw active service in the Malayan jungle against terrorists where its rocket strikes were judged to have been most successful. Hornets equipped four home-based and three overseas squadrons and were finally replaced in front-line service in June 1955. The last Hornet variant in production was the fighter-reconnaissance FR.4, of which twelve were built out of a total of 204 delivered to the RAF.

Above: these two Hornet F.3s, are from No 19 Squadron, based at Church Fenton, in May 1950.

Handley Page Hastings

The Handley Page Hastings served with the RAF as a long-range transport, carrying either thirty paratroops and their equipment, or fifty normally equipped troops. This York replacement was designed to Air Ministry specification C.3/44 and the first prototype flew at Wittering for the first time in May 1946. The first Transport Command Squadron to be equipped with the Hastings C.1 was No 47 Squadron, based at Dishforth, which received its aircraft during October 1948. The Hastings C.2, with more powerful engines, increased fuel capacity and re-designed tail assembly, was introduced in late 1950. Total Hastings production, which ended in October 1952, amounted to 146 aircraft.

The type was withdrawn from trunk routes with the arrival of Bristol Britannias in 1959 and was switched instead to tactical transport operations, remaining in service as late as the end of 1967.

1949-1958

Bristol Brigand

The Bristol Brigand was originally conceived as a Beaufighter replacement with a crew of three and powered by twin Bristol Hercules VIII engines, designed to specification H.7/42. The outcome was the Brigand TF.1 which was issued to Nos 36 and 42 Squadrons, Coastal Command. With the end of the war the Air Staff decided that there was no longer a requirement for a torpedo bomber

in the RAF and the aircraft were recalled for rebuilding as bombers.

The Brigand B.1 first entered service with No 84 Squadron, based at Habbaniya, Iraq, early in 1949 and during its career the Brigand B.1 served exclusively in the Middle and Far East, equipping only three squadrons. From 1950 to 1954 Brigands operated extensively against the terrorists in Malaya, armed with four nose-

mounted 20-mm Hispano cannon and with provision for up to 2,000 lb of under-wing stores. Powered by two 2,470-hp Bristol Centaurus 57 engines, the Brigand B.1 was capable of a top speed of 358 mph at 16,000 ft.

Brigands were also produced as meterological reconnaissance variants and, as the T.4 and T.5, for initial instruction of radar navigators, in which role they first

equipped No 228 OCU at Leeming in July 1951. The RAF received a total of 143 Brigands, the last of which was retired in March 1958.

Top: the first production Brigand TF.1 with long-range drop tanks. Airborne is another TF.1 with rockets and centre-line torpedo (below) before conversion to bomber configuration. Photographed in September 1947.

de Havilland Chipmunk T.10

The two-seat de Havilland Chipmunk T.10, which originated from the company's Canadian branch in Toronto, first flew in May 1946 and was adopted by the RAF for use by University Air Squadrons in February 1950, superseding the venerable Tiger Moth. It was also used in the Reserve Flying Schools of the RAF Volunteer Reserve until their closure in 1952-53. The Chipmunk was also used operationally, albeit briefly, by No 114 Squadron in Cyprus for internal security duties during disturbances in 1958. From 1973, with the introduction of the Scottish Aviation Bulldog as the RAF's standard primary trainer, the Gipsy Major-engined Chipmunk was gradually withdrawn from service.

Westland Dragonfly

The Westland Dragonfly was a licence-built version of the American Sikorsky S-51 helicopter and entered service with the RAF as the HC.2 in 1950. The improved HC.4, with metal rotor-blades in place of the composite blades of the HC.2, first entered RAF service in 1952 and in February 1953 the RAF's first helicopter squadron, No 194, was formed from the Malayan Casualty Evacuation Flight.

Accommodation in the HC.4 was for a pilot and three passengers or two strethcer cases in enclosed paniers mounted outside the fuselage. The Dragonfly was finally withdrawn from the Far east Air Force in June 1956.

Powered by a 550-hp Alvis Leonides 50 engine, the HC.4 had a maximum speed of 103 mph at sea level and cruised at 83 mph.

Boeing Washington

The huge Boeing Washington was supplied to the RAF under an American Military Aid Programme in 1950 to supplement the over-stretched Lincolns in No 3 Group. Originally ex-USAF B-29A Super-fortresses, the RAF eventually took delivery of eighty-eight Washingtons, the first of which were issued to No 149 Squadron at Coningsby in November 1950. In 1952 No 90 Squadron's Washingtons won the Lawrence Minot Trophy for bombing efficiency, and in the following year the Trophy went to Washingtons of No 115 Squadron.

With the introduction of Canberras into Bomber Command in the early 1950s the Washingtons were gradually made redundant and by the end of 1954 most Bomber Command aircraft had returned to the United States, although a few remained with Signals Command until early in 1958.

Powered by four 2,200-hp Wright Cyclone Eighteen R-3350 engines, the Washington B.1 was capable of a top speed of 350 mph at 25,000 ft and could carry a bomb load of 6,000 lb for 3,000 miles.

This Washington is from No 207 Squadron based at Marham, photographed in November 1952.

Vickers Valetta

The Vickers Valetta C.1 was a military version of the Viking airliner, designed to Air Ministry specification C.9/46, and was fitted out for troop carrying (with thirty-four troops, or twenty paratroops), freight lifting, glider towing, supply dropping and air ambulance duties. The first Valetta C.1 production aircraft flew in January 1948. The C.2 was fitted out as a VIP transport with capacity for nine to fifteen passengers.

The Valetta T.3 'flying class-room' version was produced to specification T.1/49 for training navigators. It first flew in August 1950 and some forty of this type were to equip Nos 1 and 2 Air Navigation Schools and the RAF College, Cranwell.

The last Valetta was retired from RAF service in the Summer of 1969 when Valleta C.2 VX 573 left RAF Wildenrath in Germany to join the other historic aircraft in the RAF Museum at Hendon.

Vickers Varsity

Not dissimilar in general outline to the Valetta, the Vickers Varsity T.1 was designed as an advanced trainer for pilots destined to fly heavy piston-engined transports. Unlike the Valetta, the larger Varsity was fitted with a tricycle under-carriage and its long range, a maximum of 2,648 miles, enabled it to be used for long-distance training flights.

First deliveries were to No 201 Advanced Flying School at Swinderby, Lincolnshire, in October 1951, where it replaced Wellingtons. In 1960, a new scheme of pilot training was evolved in which those pilots who had qualified on Jet Provosts and who were intended for propeller-driven aircraft such as the Britannia or Shackleton, converted on Varsities at RAF Valley. Varsities were also used for navigator training and from 1970 this activity was concentrated at RAF Finningley, home of No 6 FTS. It was a Varsity from this unit that flew the aircraft's sortie with the RAF, on April 2, 1976.

Armstrong Whitworth Meteor NF.11

The Armstrong Whitworth Meteor NF.11, designed to Air Ministry specification F.24/28, was a logical development of the Meteor day fighter series and was produced to fill the requirement for a jet night fighter to replace the Mosquito NF variants, which had been in service since the war years. The Meteor night fighters were characterised by their long noses, which housed the radar and an additional seat for the navigator, and combined the long-span wings of the early day fighters with the squared-off tail assembly of the F.8.

The first production NF.11 flew for the first time on November 13, 1950 and the first squadron to receive the type was No 29 Squadron at Tangmere, in January 1951. The NF.11 had its four 20-mm cannon mounted in the wings since the nose was occupied by radar equipment and, powered by a pair of 3,600-lb thrust Rolls-Royce Derwent 8 turbojets, had a top speed of 579 mph at 9,842 ft and a service ceiling of 43,000 ft.

The NF.11 was followed into service by the NF.12 with improved radar, the first of which flew in April 1953. The NF.13 was a tropicalised version for service in the Middle East. The final production variant was the NF.14 with a clear-view canopy and lengthened fuselage, which first flew in October 1953. Total production of Meteor night fighters amounted to 547, consisting of 307 NF.11s, 100 NF.12s, 40 NF.13s and 100 NF.14s.

The NF.14 hung on in front-line service until as late as 1961 when No 60 Squadron of the Far East Air Force finally exchanged its Meteors for Javelins, but some modified NF.14s, re-designated NF.(T)14 to indicate their training role, remained in service with Air Navigation Schools until superseded by the Dominie in 1965.
Below: a pair of NF.11s of No 29 Squadron, photographed in June 1953. The NF.14 was photographed in May 1957 and is probably from No 153 Squadron.

English Electric Canberra
B.2/PR.3

The English Electric Canberra was the first jet bomber to enter service with the RAF, No 101 Squadron at Binbrook receiving its first B.2s in May 1951. The B.2 carried a crew of three and was capable of carrying up to 6,000 lb of bombs in its internal bomb bay. Production totalled 430 aircraft.

An improved version, the B.6, began equipping Bomber Command in June 1954. Both B.2 and B.6 Canberras were operational during the Anglo-French violation of Suez in 1956, the B.2s operating out of Cyprus and the B.6s from both Cyprus and Malta. With the building up of the V-force the Canberra's role with Bomber Command became of secondary importance and the type was switched instead to the tactical nuclear strike role in support of CENTO forces in the Near and Far East. The last Canberra left Bomber Command in 1961.

The photo-reconnaissance variants were a logical development of the light bombers already in service, and the first PR.3 entered service with No 540 Squadron at Benson in 1953. The PR.3 was followed by the PR.7, which was a photo-reconnaissance version of the B.6. Final variant in the series was the PR.9, which first flew in July 1958, equipping No 58 Squadron at Wyton in the spring of 1960. This was the high altitude version and had a new, long-span wing of increased chord at the centre section inboard of the engines. Total production was twenty-three aircraft, all built by Shorts.

Left: Canberra B.2s from No 100 Squadron, based at Wittering, photographed in May 1955. Above left: WD933 was the prototype Sapphire 7-engined aircraft, photographed in September 1954.

Boulton Paul Balliol

The Boulton Paul Balliol two-seat advanced trainer was originally conceived as a replacement for the Harvard to specification T.14/47, and four Merlin-engined prototypes were built, the first flying in July 1948. Large production contracts for the Balliol T.2 were placed, only to be cut back when, in 1951, further changes in training policy advocated the introduction of pure jets for advanced instruction. Nevertheless, the Balliol was produced, a total of 162 being built, and the type equipped No 7 Flying School at Cottesmore as well as the RAF College, Cranwell.

Top: prototype Balliol T.1 with the Bristol Mercury 30 engine in 1947. Right: VR596 was a Balliol T.2 and was later fitted with an arrester hook for carrier trials.

Lockheed Neptune

Lockheed Neptunes equipped the RAF from 1952 to 1957 and were equivalent to the US Navy's P2V-5s. Carrying a crew of seven, they were used for maritime reconnaisance until replaced by Shackletons.

The first fifty-two aircraft arrived at St Eval, Cornwall, in January 1952 and entered service with Nos 36, 203, 210 and 217 Squadrons. Many RAF aircraft were modified to have clear plexiglass noses without guns and a lengthened tail containing MAD (Magnetic Anomoly Detector) gear. Four specially modified Neptunes were also operated by No 1453 Flight, based at Topcliffe, on airborne early warning duties from November 1952 to June 1956.

Powered by two 3,250-hp Wright Turbo-Cyclone engines, the Neptune had a top speed of 363mph at 9,500ft and a maximum bomb load of 8,000lb.

Bristol Sycamore

The Bristol Sycamore search and rescue helicopter was developed from the Bristol Type 171 Mk 1, which first flew in July 1947. The first prototype aircraft were powered by a Pratt & Whitney Wasp Junior engine, but all production aircraft, both civil and military, were fitted with the 550-hp Alvis Leonides 73 engine.

The first RAF variant was the HR.12 search and rescue helicopter, the first of which was delivered to St Mawgan for trials in February 1952. The major production variant for the RAF, however, was the HR.14, of which the RAF took delivery of about ninety, based at Chivenor, Leuchars, Horsham St Faith, North Coates and Thornaby. The Sycamore was also used by three overseas squadrons, in Malaya and in Cyprus. Maximum speed at sea level was 127 mph and cruising speed was 105 mph.

de Havilland Vampire T.11

The de Havilland Vampire T.11 marked the beginning of a new era in pilot training in which RAF pilots qualified for their 'wings' on jet aircraft after basic training on Hunting Percival Provost aircraft. The prototype first flew in November 1950 and the type first entered service with the Advanced Flying Schools at Valley and Weston Zoyland in 1952, and with the Fighter Weapons School at Leconfield. They were also issued to No 5 FTS at Oakington in 1954 and in 1956 became the first jet trainer to be used by the RAF College, Cranwell. Oakington was the first unit to operate the Vampire T.11 as the second part of the new Provost/Vampire training sequence, that part of the syllabus consisting of 110 hours of advanced training.

By 1965, the RAF's only active Vampire trainers were at No 1 FTS at Linton-on-Ouse and in January 1966 these were transferred to No 7 FTS, Church Fenton and thence to No 3 FTS Leeming, where they flew their last sortie in November 1967. A few remained with the Central Air Traffic Control School at Shawbury until 1970, and with No 3 Civilian Army Co-operation Unit at Exeter until 1971.

Powered by a single 3,500-lb thrust de Havilland Goblin 35 turbojet, the Vampire T.11 had a top speed of 549mph at 20,000ft. Left: a pair of Vampire T.11s is seen here led by a Venom FB.5, photographed in April 1956. The three T.11s (below) are from the OCU at Merryfield early in 1953.

131

de Havilland Venom

The de Havilland Venom was built
in two main versions: as a single-
seat fighter-bomber, armed with
four 20-mm cannon in the nose
and provision for 2,000 lb of bomb
or rocket projectiles; or as a two-
seat night-fighter with AI radar and
armed with four nose-mounted
cannon.

The first prototype Venom flew
at Hatfield for the first time in
September 1949 and, although production contracts were cut back,
more than 350 Venom FB.1s were
built and the type equipped several
squadrons with the 2nd TAF in
Germany from 1953 to 1955, the
first to be equipped being No 11 in
August 1952. From February
1954, Venom FB.1s replaced
Vampires in the Middle East Air
Force and in the following year an
improved version, the FB.4, was
introduced with power-operated
ailerons, ejector seat and re-
designed tail surfaces. The last
Venom fighter-bombers were
those of No 28 Squadron, FEAF,
which were retired in July 1962.

The two-seat night-fighter ver-
sion was a development of the
FB.1 and the first NF.2s reached
the RAF in 1953, first equipping
No 23 Squadron at Coltishall. The
last version to go into service was
the NF.3, the first of which reached
No 141 Squadron in June 1955.
Total Venom production for the
RAF was 712 aircraft.

Right: originally built as a Vampire FB.5, VV613 became the prototype Venom F.1. Below, a
Venom NF.2 photographed in September 1952.

Candair Sabre

The RAF was supplied with some 430 Candair-built F-86E Sabres after it had declared its anxiety over its lack of swept-wing transonic fighters in the early 1950s. The first aircraft were Sabre Mk 2s and began to reach Britain in late 1952, but the majority of the 430 aircraft was made up of Sabre Mk 4s, which re-equipped No 3, 4, 20, 26, 67, 71, 93, 112, 130 and 234 Squadrons with the 2nd Tactical Air Force in Germany, and Nos 66 and 92 Squadrons of Fighter Command. By the end of June 1956 all the Sabres in Germany had finally been superseded by Hunters.

Powered by a 5,200-lb thrust General Electric J-47 GE-13 engine, the Sabre F.4 had a maximum speed of 670 mph and was armed with six .50-calibre guns.

Left: these Sabre F.4s are from No 92 Squadron, based at Linton-on-Ouse between January 1954 and April 1956. Below: Sabre F.4s from RAF Brüggen, West Germany, September 1954.

Hunting Percival Provost

The Provost two-seat basic trainer was designed to Air Ministry specification T.16/48 and the prototype first flew in February 1950. A production contract for 200 was placed in February 1951. With the introduction of the Provost in 1953, the RAF was able to begin its Provost/Vampire pilot training scheme. Pupil and instructor were seated side-by-side and, powered by a 550-hp Alvis Leonides 126 engine, the Provost T.1 had a top speed of 200 mph at sea level, cruising at 162 mph at 5,000ft.

First deliveries were to the Central Flying School's Basic Training Squadron at South Cerney, and in 1954 the type entered service with the RAF College, Cranwell. More than 380 were built, the last in April 1956, and with the introduction of the Jet Provost, the Provost T.1 was gradually withdrawn from use, the last school to be equipped, No 6 FTS at Ternhill, converting to the new jet type after its move to Acklington in August 1961.

These Provost T.1s are from No 6 FTS at Ternhill, March 1954.

Scottish Aviation Pioneer

The Pioneer CC.1 was a five-seat casualty evacuation and communications aircraft which first flew in June 1950. It was specifically designed for operation from short, confined landing strips and with its full-span controlled leading edge slats and large area Fowler-type flaps the take-off run was 75 yards and the landing run could be restricted to only 66 yards. Entering service in August 1953, a total of forty was supplied to the RAF before production ended in 1957; squadrons equipped included Nos 20, 78, 209 and 230. The first to receive the Pioneer was No 267 (later re-numbered 209) and this unit was to be actively involved in Operation Firedog against the Malaysian terrorists.

The Pioneer was powered by a 520-hp Alvis Leonides 502 engine which gave the type a top speed of 145 mph at 1,500 ft and a cruising speed of 114 mph at 5,000 ft.

Hunting Percival Pembroke

The Pembroke C.1 eight-seat communications aircraft was derived from the civil Prince feeder-liner and first flew in November 1952. A total of forty-six Pembrokes was ordered for the RAF, but two were diverted to the (then) Royal Rhodesian Air Force. Production ended in February 1958. In the Autumn of 1956, six Pembrokes modified for photo-reconnaissance were delivered to No 81 Squadron in Malaya.

After a re-sparring programme undertaken by BAC from 1970, some fourteen Pembrokes still remain in RAF service, serving only with No 60 Squadron at RAF Wildenrath, Germany.

Powered by two 550-hp Alvis Leonides 127 engines, the Pembroke has a maximum speed of 224 mph at 2,000 ft, cruising at 155 mph at 8,000 ft. Maximum range is 1,160 miles.

Hawker Hunter

Another of those rare aircraft that are as delightful to fly as they are to look at, the Hunter was produced to meet Air Ministry specification F.3/48 for a Meteor replacement, issued in March 1948. Three prototypes were ordered in June of that year, the first of which flew at Boscombe Down in July 1951. The first production Hunter F.1 was flown from Dunsfold in May 1953, but entry into service was delayed by Ministry insistence that an air-brake be fitted and No 43 Squadron, based at Leuchars, did not receive its Hunters until the end of July 1954. The only other squadrons to be equipped with F.1s were Nos 54, based at Odiham, and No 222, also at Leuchars, many of the remaining F.1s being issued to Operational Conversion units. A total of 139 F.1s was built at Kingston and Blackpool.

The Sapphire-powered F.2 was not affected by the engine-surge problems that had attended the F.1 when it fired its guns, and this variant, built by Armstrong Whitworth at Coventry, entered service with Nos 257 and 263 Squadrons at

Wattisham at the end of 1954. Only forty-five were built before attention was switched to the F.4. The Hunter F.3 was the designation given to the Hunter prototype, WB188, in 1953 after it had been fitted with a re-heated Rolls-Royce Avon RA.7R engine.

The Hunter F.4 entered service with Nos 54 and 111 Squadrons in March 1955 and introduced increased internal fuel capacity and provision for a wide variety of under-wing stores. By 1956 the F.4 equipped some thirteen squadrons of the 2nd TAF in Germany as well as seven home-based squadrons, replacing Meteor 8s and Venoms. A total of 365 Hunter 4s was built by both Hawker factories, to be followed by 105 Armstrong Whitworth-built F.5s, fitted with the Armstrong Siddeley Sapphire engine.

The Hunter F.6 was virtually a new aircraft, fitted with the 10,000-lb thrust Avon 203, all-flying tailplane and 'saw-tooth' leading edge. It first entered service with No 74 Squadron in 1956 and by 1958 all RAF day fighter squad-

rons in Europe had been re-equipped with the F.6, and in March of that year No 208 Squadron was re-formed with F.6s and posted to the Middle East Air Force in Cyprus. The F.6 also ushered in the era of the famous Hunter-equipped aerobatic teams: the Black Arrows of No 111 Squadron and the Blue Diamonds of No 92 Squadron.

The arrival at Fighter Command of the Lightning F.2 in 1962 signalled the rapid withdrawal from front-line service of the Hunter F.6, and in December that year the last F.6 was also withdrawn from Germany with the conversion of No 14 Squadron to the Canberra B.(I)8.

Powered by the 10,000-lb thrust Rolls-Royce Avon 203, the F.6 had a top speed of 715 mph at sea level or Mach 0.95 at 36,000 ft. In addition to its armament of four 30-mm Aden cannon in a removable pack, the Hunter F.6 had provision for two 1,000-lb bombs, two 100-gal Napalm tanks or 2-in rocket batteries on the inner pylons and 3-in RPs on the outer pylons.

Supermarine Swift

The Swift fighters were not successful in RAF service. With a lineage stretching back to the Spitfire, by way of the Spiteful, Attacker, Type 510 and Type 535, it should have been a winner, but from the start it was an aircraft beset by all sorts of problems and only one squadron, No 56, was to use it as a front-line interceptor.

Two prototypes and 100 production aircraft were ordered in November 1950 as insurance against the failure of the Hunter, ordered the previous month, and the first production F.1 flew in August 1952. In February 1954, No 56 Squadron received its first Swift F.1s, and became the first RAF squadron to be equipped with a British-built swept-wing fighter. The F.1 was armed with 30-mm Aden Cannon and had a fixed tailplane and no re-heat. It was followed into service in August 1952 by the F.2 which differed by having four cannon and a cranked wing lading edge. The F.3 was similar to the F.2 but was fitted with re-heat, and the F.4 incorporated variable-incidence tailplane; neither variant was to enter service because the whole Swift fighter proramme was cancelled in February 1955 after twenty F.1s and sixteen F.2s had been delivered.

Powered by a 7,500-lb thrust Rolls-Royce Avon 105 turbojet the Swift F.1 had a maximum speed of 690 mph, while the record-breaking Swift F.4 prototype raised the World Air Speed Record to 737.7 mph in September 1953.

Left: a Swift F.3, photographed in September 1954. Below: all dressed up and nowhere to go. Swift F.3s awaiting delivery to the RAF.

Westland Whirlwind HAR.2

The Whirlwind is the British-built version of the American Sikorsky S-55 and was operated by both the Royal Navy and the RAF, the first RAF version being the HAR.2 which began service with Coastal Command's search and rescue organisation in February 1955 when it equipped No 22 Squadron, based at Thorney Island. The Whirlwind was also used by Transport Command as a communications aircraft, and in April 1955 it was announced that two Whirlwinds were to be added to the Queen's Flight.

Powered by a 600-hp Pratt & Whitney R-1340-40 engine, the Whirlwind HAR.2 had a maximum speed of 110 mph at sea level, cruising at 85 mph.

The Whirlwind HAR.10, which first flew in 1961, is equipped with the 1,050-hp Rolls-Royce Bristol Gnome H 100 gas turbine engine. These elderly helicopters, many of which were converted from Mks 2 or 4, still serve in the search and rescue role with No 202 Squadron, dispersed at various sites in Britain and a few are still used for communications. Cruising speed is 104 mph and range with ten passengers is 108 miles.

Vickers Valiant B.1

The first of Bomber Command's trio of V-bombers to enter service, the Valiant B.1 replaced the Canberras and Lincolns of No 3 Group, and the total of 104 aircraft built equipped Nos 7, 18, 49, 90, 138, 148, 199, 207, 214 and 543 Squadrons. Designed to Air Ministry specification B.9/48, the prototype Valiant first flew in May 1951 powered by four 6,500-lb thrust Avon RA.3 engines. The first of five pre-production aircraft flew at Brooklands in December 1953, and the first Valiant squadron to be formed was No 138, at Gaydon in January 1955.

The Valiant B.1s were followed into service by a long-range strategic reconnaissance version, the B (PR) 1, which was itself followed by a multi-purpose version capable of operating as a flight refuelling tanker as well as bomber and reconnaissance aircraft. A total of forty-five aircraft were equipped as bomber/tankers. All Valiants were withdrawn from service in January 1965 and subsequently scrapped following the discovery of metal fatigue in the airframes, a condition probably aggravated by the switching of the Valiant to the low-level role early in 1964, in common with the other V-bombers.

Powered by four 10,000-lb thrust Rolls-Royce Avon 201 turbojets, the Valiant B.1 had a maximum speed of 567 mph at 30,000 ft, a maximum range of 4,500 miles and a service ceiling of 54,000 ft. Capable of carrying a nuclear weapon, the Valiant's bomb load was 21,000 lb.

Gloster Javelin

Designed to Air Ministry specification F.4/48, the Javelin was the first British aircraft designed specifically as an all-weather and night-fighter, and the first prototype of this large two-seat delta-winged aircraft flew from Moreton Valence for the first time in November 1951. Deliveries of the first FAW.1s to No 46 Squadron at Odiham took place in February 1956, the AI.10 radar-equipped aircraft being powered by two Bristol Siddeley Sapphire 102s. A total of forty FAW.1s was built, the second squadron to be equipped being No 87 in Germany.

The FAW.2 differed in being powered by the more powerful 8,300-lb Sapphire engines and carried the American Westinghouse APQ-43 radar in a slightly shorter nose. The Mk 3 was a two-seat dual-control trainer and served mainly with No 228 OCU at Leeming from October 1957 to August 1961.

The FAW.4 incorporated an all-moving tailplane and first equipped Nos 23 and 141 Squadrons at the beginning of 1957. A total of fifty of this version was built. The FAW.5 was generally similar to the Mk 4 but had increased internal fuel tankage and the thirty-three FAW.6s built were basically Mk 5s with the American radar. First deliveries to No 89 Squadron were in 1958.

Availability of the much more powerful 200 Series Sapphire engine resulted in extensive re-engineering of the Javelin, with increased wing fuel tankage, more advanced AI radar and primary armament changed from guns to the infra-red homing Firestreak missile. Other modifications included a lengthened rear fuselage, the incorporation of vortex generators on the wings and thickened aileron trailing edges. First of the new versions was the FAW.7 which first equipped No 33 Squadron in August 1958. The FAW.8 was the final production variant and first entered service with No 41 Squadron in 1959. It differed from the Mk 7 only in having an American radar, drooped wing leading edge, Sperry autopilot and modified afterburner system. The FAW.9s were simply forty-six Mk 7s brought up to Mk 8 standard. The first conversion flew in May 1959 and a total of 385 Javelins of all Marks was built for the RAF.

The last Javelins were withdrawn from RAF service when No 60 Squadron at Tengah was disbanded in April 1968. Powered by two 11,000-lb thrust Bristol Siddeley Sapphire 203s the FAW.9 had a maximum speed of 620 mph at 40,000 ft.

Equipped with four Firestreak mock-ups is this FAW.2, while (inset) carrying the real thing are these FAW.9s from No 25 Squadron.

Supermarine Swift FR.5

The Swift FR.5 differed from the earlier, fighter versions in having a lengthened nose housing three F95 cameras, one mounted in the extreme nose and two just ahead of the air intakes for oblique photography. Like the abandoned F.4, the PR.5 had the taller fin, frameless canopy and a centre-line rack for a 220-gal fuel tank. First flight was in May 1955 and deliveries to Nos 2 and 79 Squadrons of the 2nd TAF in Germany began in 1956. As a photo-reconnaissance aircraft, the Swift was fairly successful, and FR.5s won the NATO reconnaissance competition in 1957 and 1959, but it had a prodigious fuel consumption for its somewhat indifferent performance. Powered by a 7,715-lb thrust (9,450-lb with re-heat) Rolls-Royce Avon 114 turbojet, the FR.5 had a maximum speed of 685 mph at sea level and a range of 480 miles.

The FR.5 remained in service with the RAF in Germany until the summer of 1961 when it was finally replaced by the Hunter FR.10.

Blackburn Beverley C.1

The Beverley was a development of General Aircraft's GAL.60 Universal Freighter Mk 1, which first flew in June 1950, and differed from the Universal Freighter in having four 2,850-hp Bristol Centaurus 273 engines in place of the original Hercules, and the introduction of clam-shell doors and an enlarged tail boom. Performance was correspondingly improved.

The Beverley C.1 first entered service with Transport Command in March 1956, equipping No 47 Squadron at Abingdon. It later equipped No 30 and 53 Squadrons in Britain, No 84 Squadron in the Middle East and No 34 Squadron in the Far East. Production ended in May 1958 after forty-seven had been built for the RAF and the type was finally withdrawn from service at the end of 1967. Maximum speed was 238 mph at 5,700 ft and payload was almost 22 tons.

English Electric Canberra B.(I)8

The Canberra B.(I)8 was a two-seat long-range night intruder or high-altitude bomber. The prototype B.8 first flew in July 1954 and differed from earlier Canberras in having a clear-view canopy set on the port-side of the nose with the navigator/bomb-aimer in the nose. In its intruder role the Canberra B.(I)8 was armed with a pack of four 20-mm Hispano cannon located in the rear of the weapons bay, leaving room in the forward part for sixteen 4.5-in flares or three 1,000-lb bombs. During 1963 the type was modified to carry two Nord AS.30 air-to-surface missiles.

The first of seventy-four production aircraft first flew in June 1955 and equipped No 88 Squadron in Germany in May 1956. Later, B.(I)8s equipped Nos 3, 14, 16 and 213 Squadrons, the last aircraft to remain in service being those of No 16 Squadron at Laarbruch in Germany which disbanded in June 1972.

Powered by two 7,400-lb thrust Rolls-Royce Avon 109s the Canberra Mk 8 had a maximum speed of 517 mph at sea level and 541 mph at 40,000 ft. Maximum range was 805 miles with full bomb load.

Avro Shackleton MR.3

The Shackleton was evolved to meet the requirements of specification R.5/46 for a maritime reconnaissance aircraft and utilised the basic wing structure of the Lincoln bomber which was mated to an entirely new fuselage and Griffon engines driving six-bladed contra-rotating propellers. The first of three prototypes was flown in March 1949 and deliveries to Coastal Command of the first MR.1s began in 1951. The MR.2 was introduced late in 1952 and featured a re-positioned radar, re-designed nose, deletion of the tail turret and its replacement by a tapered, transparent cone for observation. The new ventral radome permitted an uninterrupted 360° scan.

The Shackleton MR.3 was the final production version and introduced a tricycle undercarriage, reworked flight deck and new wing outer panels with tip tanks to increase still further its already impressive range. The first MR.3 flew in September 1955 but deliveries did not begin for a further eighteen months, in 1957, when No 220 Squadron was re-

equipped. A total of thirty-four MR.3s was delivered to the RAF, equipping Nos 42, 120, 201, 203, 206 and 220 Squadrons.

Originally powered by just four 2,455-hp Rolls-Royce Griffon 57A engines, Shackleton MR.3s were modernized from 1966 with the

addition of two 2,500-lb thrust Bristol Siddeley Viper turbojets in the outer nacelles. With the arrival of the Nimrod in Strike Command from 1970, the Shackletons were progressively withdrawn from service.

Right: this Shackleton MR.1 of

No 269 Squadron RAF Ballykelly, was photographed in March 1958. The MR.2 (above) was photographed in Saudi Arabia in February 1965.

Avro Vulcan B.1

The Vulcan was Avro's answer to Air Ministry specification B.35/46, issued in January 1947, and was the first large bomber in the world to adopt the delta wing plan-form. The prototype, powered by four 6,500-lb Rolls-Royce Avons, first flew in August 1952 and it was immediately apparent that the Vulcan was going to be a winner, with almost fighter-like manoeuvrability. Production aircraft were to be powered by the vastly more powerful Bristol Olympus 101, and the first of these flew in February 1955; the second production aircraft startled spectators at that year's Farnborough Air Show by executing a perfect slow roll, when flown by the irrepressible Roly Falk.

The Vulcan first entered service with No 83 Squadron, Bomber Command, in July 1957, and subsequently served with Nos 27, 44, 50, 60, 61, 101 and 617 Squadrons. In 1961, some B.1s were modified to carry electronic countermeasures equipment in a new bulged rear fuselage and were re-designated Vulcan B.1As. Production of B.1s totalled forty-five aircraft and ended in April 1959.

Although performance details have never been released officially, a reasonable guess would put the Vulcan B.1's maximum speed at about 620 mph at altitude with a service ceiling of about 55,000 ft. Bomb load was at least twenty-one 1,000-lb bombs, or nuclear bombs.

Handley Page Victor B.1

Designed to meet the same Air Ministry specification as the Vulcan (B.35/46), the crescent-wing Victor B.1 was the last of the three V-bombers to enter service with the RAF. The prototype first flew in December 1952 but development took so long that the production Victor B.1 did not enter service with Bomber Command until No 10 Squadron at Cottesmore received its aircraft in April 1958, by which time the original concept of a bomber capable of flying fast and high enough so as to be immune to attack was redundant.

On being superseded in front-line bomber squadrons by the Victor B.2, the original B.1s were converted to tanker aircraft for in-flight refuelling and re-designated Victor K.1A. They were supplied to Nos 55, 57 and 214 Squadrons and first entered service in 1965.

Powered by four 11,000-lb thrust Bristol Siddeley Sapphire 202 turbojets, the Victor B.1 had a maximum speed of about 640 mph at altitude and a service ceiling of 55,000 ft.

Scottish Aviation Twin Pioneer

The Twin-Pioneer general-purpose aircraft was used for troop, paratroop and freight transport, casualty evacuation, photographic survey, supply dropping and even light bombing roles. They have also been equipped with speech broadcast equipment, anti-tank missiles and machine guns. The first military example flew in August 1957 and a total of thirty-nine was built, the last of which was delivered in March 1961.

The 'Twin-Pin' inherited the STOL characteristics of the earlier single-engined Pioneer and operated with distinction from the roughest strips in many parts of the world, including Aden, Kuwait, Bahrain and Borneo. The type was finally withdrawn from front-line service at the end of 1968 after equipping Nos 225 and 230 Squadrons in Britain, No 78 Squadron in Aden, Nos 21 and 152 Squadrons in Bahrein, No 21 Squadron in Kenya and No 209 Squadron in the Far East.

Powered by two 550-hp Alvis Leonides engines, the Twin Pioneer CC.1 had a maximum speed of 165 mph at 2,000 ft and a range with sixteen passengers, of 398 miles.

Hawker Hunter T.7

The Hunter T.7 two-seat trainer started as a private venture in 1953, progressing through the P.1101 design of 1954, tendered to meet specification T.157D. Based on the Hunter F.4 with an Avon 113 turbojet, the prototype P.1101 first flew in July 1955, but because of airflow instability problems around the hood, necessitating a lengthy trials period with various hood and fairing shapes, the first production T.7 did not fly until October 1957. Production orders totalled forty-five aircraft for the RAF, the first of which reached No 229 Operational Conversion Unit at RAF Chivenor, in 1958. Hunter T.7s were later issued to almost every operational Hunter squadron for instrument training and continuation flying.

Powered by the 8,000-lb thrust Rolls-Royce Avon turbojet, the Hunter T.7, a few of which are still operated by No 4 Flying Training School at Valley and by the Tactical Weapons Unit at Brawdy, has a maximum speed of Mach 0.92 at 36,000 ft.

1959-1968

BAC Jet Provost T.3 and T.4

The BAC (formerly Hunting P.84) Jet Provost two-seat basic trainer is a direct descendant of the Leonides-engined Provost in that the same overall shape was retained wherever possible in order to reproduce the good handling qualities of the earlier aircraft. The first T.3, which was to become the standard jet trainer for the RAF for several years, made its first flight in June 1958, deliveries commencing almost exactly a year later. The first unit to receive the T.3 was No 2 Flying Training School at Syerston, with the first course beginning in October 1959.

The T.4, with the more powerful Viper 202 engine, entered service with flying training schools in November 1961, and when production ended in mid-1964 more than 185 had been delivered, equipping Nos 1, 2, 3, 6 and 7 FTS, the Central Flying School at Little Rissington, the College of Air Warfare, Manby and the RAF College, Cranwell. Under a three-year modernisation programme undertaken by BAC at Warton which ended in mid-1976, a number of T.3s were upgraded to T.3A status by the addition of new avionics equipment and a revised panel layout; these aircraft are currently operated by No 1 FTS as Linton-on-Ouse and the RAF College, Cranwell.

These T.3s from the Flying Training School at Syerston were photographed in July 1960.

Bristol Britannia

Cancellation of the Vickers V.1000 pure jet transport for the RAF in 1955 led to the decision to order a military version of the turbo-prop Britannia in its place. Six C.1s were ordered initially in January 1956, the first of which made its first flight in December 1958, by which time orders had been increased to twenty aircraft. These were subsequently joined by three Britannia C.2s.

First squadron to receive the Britannia was No 99, stationed at Lyneham, Wiltshire, in June 1959, followed by No 511 Squadron in December of that year. Britannias gave excellent service during their relatively long career with the RAF and for a time formed the spearhead of Transport (later Air Support) Command's long-range strategic transport fleet.

Powered by four 4,445-hp Bristol Siddeley Proteus 255 engines, the Britannia C.1 had a cruising speed of 360 mph and a range with its maximum payload of 37,400 lb of 4,310 miles. Following defence economies, the Britannia was withdrawn from service in January 1976 with the disbandment of Nos 99 and 511 Squadrons.

Hawker Hunter FGA.9

The ground-attack Hunter FGA.9, which formed the major part of Fighter Command's close-support force during the 1960s, was not a new aircraft at all but a conversion of the F.6. Originally intended for service exclusively in the Middle East as a Venom replacement, modifications included the installation of a tail parachute, the addition of 230-gal drop tanks and extra stations beneath the wings for ground-attack stores. Deliveries to the RAF began in October 1959 with the re-equipping of No 8 Squadron, based at Khormaksar, Aden.

With the disappearance of Fighter Command and the formation of Strike Command in April 1968, the tactical support and strike force in the UK was vested in two FGA.9 Squadrons, Nos 1 and 54. The last operational FGA.9s in the RAF were those of No 8 Squadron, which returned from the Far East to disband at the end of 1971. A few remain as trainers at RAF Valley and at the Tactical Weapons Unit, Brawdy but will shortly be replaced by Hawker Siddeley Hawks.

The Hunter FR.10 was also based on the F.6 and was produced as a Swift FR.5 replacement for the 2nd TAF in Germany, the first aircraft flying in November 1958. It carried one forward facing and two oblique cameras in the nose, while retaining normal armament. The first unit to be equipped was No 2 Squadron in 1960, followed by No 4 Squadron. These two squadrons currently operate Jaguars and Harriers, respectively.

Powered by one 10,150-lb thrust Rolls-Royce Avon 207 engine, the Hunter FGA.9 had a maximum speed of Mach 0.95 at 36,000 ft and a tactical radius with drop tanks and 2,000 lb of armament of 219 miles.

BAC Lightning F.1, F.2 and F.3

The English Electric (later BAC) Lightning was the first single-seat fighter for the RAF to exceed the speed of sound in level flight and was developed from the P.1A and P.1B, which flew in 1954 and 1957, respectively. Three P.1B prototypes were built, one of which became the first British aircraft ever to fly at Mach 2, in November 1958, followed by twenty pre-production aircraft which were used for armament, radar, systems and handling trials.

The first production Lightning F.1 made its maiden flight in October 1959 and the type first entered service with the Central Fighter Establishment at Coltishall

in December of that year; No 74 Squadron, also at Coltishall, was the first operational unit to be equipped with the F.1, in July 1960. The arrival of the Lightning at Fighter Command was a notable event as it signalled the beginning of the era of the integrated weapons system: airframe, engines, fire-control radar, armament and aircraft controls on the Lightning were all carefully co-ordinated to produce the most effective interceptor possible. Despite the misguided belief that manned aircraft were obsolete, propounded in the Defence White Paper of April 1957, development of the Lightning continued and the

F.2, with fully variable afterburner, equipped two Fighter Command squadrons, Nos 19 and 92, at Leconfield in 1963.

Between 1964 and 1966, however, the major variant was the F.3, with two Rolls-Royce Avon 301s and carrying a pair of Red Top heat-seeking missiles as an alternative to the earlier Firestreaks. The internal Aden cannon were also deleted on this variant. External changes included a new square-off fin and rudder and provision for two over-wing fuel tanks. The Lightning T.4 and T.5 are two-seat trainer versions of the F.2 and F.3, respectively.

Avro Vulcan B.2

The first production Vulcan B.2 flew in August 1958, fitted with a new wing of greater span and greater chord in the outboard sections. The new wing was also thinner and, in conjunction with the increased power of the Olympus 201 engines, gave the Vulcan B.2 a greater load carrying ability and higher ceiling (about 65,000 ft) than the earlier series. Most B.2s were equipped to carry the Blue Steel stand-off bomb, but from 1966 Vulcan B.2 squadrons were operating as low-level penetration strike aircraft using terrain-following radar and swopped their anti-radiation white paint for grey-green camouflage.

Vulcan B.2s equipped Nos 9, 27, 35, 44, 50, 83, 101 and 617 Squadrons at the formation of RAF Strike Command in April 1968, and early in 1969, Nos 9 and 35 Squadrons were to be permanently deployed in Cyprus, equipped as conventional bombers, until their return to Strike Command in 1975. Several Vulcan B.2s have since been modified to operate in the strategic reconnaissance role and are now designated Vulcan SR.2.

Westland Belvedere

Designed to meet the RAF's requirements for a medium-lift helicopter carrying both troops and freight, the Westland Belvedere HC.1 was the first twin-engined, twin-rotor helicopter to enter service with the RAF. No prototype was built, the first of twenty-six production aircraft for the RAF flying for the first time in July 1958. Three production aircraft were delivered to the trials unit in October 1960, and the Belvedere entered service with No 66 Squadron at Odiham in September 1961, later equipping Nos 26 and 72 Squadrons.

Belvederes saw service in many parts of the world during their career, notably in Tanganyika in 1963 and later in the Radfan operations. No 66 Squadron's Belvederes were active throughout the Brunei campaign from 1962 to 1966 and the type was finally retired in 1969 with the disbandment of No 66 Squadron at Seletar.

Powered by two 1,300-shp Napier Gazelle N.Ga.2 engines, the Belvedere had a maximum speed of 138 mph and a range with 6,000-lb payload of 75 miles.

de Havilland Comet 4

The first of five Comet C.4s for the RAF was delivered in February 1962 to No 216 Squadron at Lyneham, Wiltshire and differed from the earlier Comet 2s, which had reached the RAF in 1956, by having a longer fusealge accommodating ninety-four passengers instead of forty-four. The last Comets were withdrawn from RAF service with the disbanding of No 216 Squadron in June 1975.

This Comet 4C is of of No 216 Squadron and was photographed in November 1971.

Handley Page Victor B.2

The Victor B.2 was a development of the Victor Mk 1 and Mk1A, powered by four 20,600-lb thrust Rolls-Royce Conway R.Co17 Mk 201 engines. External differences included wings of greater span, enlarged air intakes, a dorsal fillet forward of the fin and a retractable scoop on each side of the fuselage close to the tail to supply ram air to two turbo-alternators for emergency power supplies. Like the Vulcan B.2, the Victor B.2BS could be armed with the Blue Steel stand-off bomb and first equipped No 139 Squadron in 1963. Low-level operations began in January 1964, the aircraft being painted in camouflage green/grey.

The Victor SR.2 was the strategic reconnaissance version and first entered service with No 543 Squadron at Wyton in the autumn of 1965. The SR.2 was not equipped to carry weapons, its bomb bay being used to accommodate a variety of cameras as well as additional fuel tankage. By the end of 1968, however, both Strike Command Victor 2 Squadrons (Nos 100 and 139) had been disbanded and sixteen of their aircraft were subsequently modified to tanker standard as Victor K.2s, replacing the K.1s at Marham. The SR.2s continued to operate until No 543 Squadron disbanded in May 1974.

The Victor B.2 had a maximum speed of Mach 0.92 at 40,000 ft and a service ceiling of about 60,000 ft. The SR.2 version was capable of radar-mapping an area the size of the Mediterranean on its own in a single seven-hour sortie.

Hawker Siddeley Gnat T.1

Development of the single-seat lightweight Gnat fighter was started as a private venture by the former Folland Aircraft company in 1951. The first Gnat prototype, powered by a Bristol Siddeley Orpheus turbojet, flew in July 1955 but the type was not adopted by the RAF as a fighter. However, it was decided instead to use it as a two-seat transonic advanced trainer and a development order for fourteen aircraft was received in 1958, total deliveries reaching 105 by 1965. The prototype flew for the first time in August 1959 and the Gnat first entered service at the Central Flying School at Little Rissington in February 1962.

From the end of 1962, when it equipped No 4 Flying Training School at Valley, the Gnat superseded the Vampire T.11 as the RAF's standard advanced trainer and although replacement by the Hawker Siddeley Hawk has begun, the type will remain in service for some time to come.

Powered by a 4,230-lb thrust Bristol Siddeley Orpheus 100 engine, the Gnat T.1 has a maximum speed of Mach 0.97 in level flight.

Hawker Siddeley Argosy

The Argosy was designed by the former Armstrong Whitworth company specifically to meet the requirements for a large-capacity civil and military passenger and freight transport and an initial production series was laid down as a private venture in the late 1950s. The RAF's version, the first of which flew in March 1961, had a re-designed fuselage with upward and downward hingeing rear loading doors which can be opened in flight for air-drop operations. The nose door was deleted and the nose fitted with weather radar. A total of 56 Argosies was ordered for the RAF, the first equipping No 114 Squadron, Transport Command in March 1962. During its career, the Argosy served with Nos 114, and 267 Squadrons of Transport (later Air Support) Command, No 115 Squadron of No 90 Group, and Nos 70, 105 and 215 Squadrons in Cyprus, the Persian Gulf and the Far East.

The Argosy had a relatively brief service life with the RAF, mainly as

a result of successive defence cut-backs and the type had virtually disappeared by the mid-1970s. A plan to convert fourteen to crew trainers was abandoned.

Powered by four 2,680-hp Rolls-Royce Dart 101 turboprops, the Argosy C.1 had a cruising speed of 269 mph at 20,000 ft and accommodated, in addition to its crew of four, either sixty-nine equipped troops, forty-eight stretcher cases or a maximum of 29,000 lb of freight.

Shown here is an Argosy E.1 radio and radar calibration aircraft from No 115 Squadron, Cottesmore, photographed in 1974.

Beagle Basset

The B.206R Basset CC.1 twin-engined light transport was originally intended for the transport of V-bomber crews, but its poor payload and range inhibited this role and the type was used instead for general communications work, the first aircraft reaching the Northern Communications Squadron at Topcliffe in the summer of 1965. Out of a total of twenty Bassets built for the RAF, nine went to the NCS; others were supplied to the Metropolitan Communications Squadron at Northolt, the Southern Communications Squadron at Bovingdon and the Western Communications Squadron at Andover. These Communications Squadrons were re-numbered from the beginning of 1969, and the last Basset was retired from No 207 Squadron in May 1974.

Westland Wessex HC.2

The Wessex is a turbine-engined development of the Sikorsky S-58 and first flew, as the HAS.1 for the Royal Navy, in May 1957. The first version for the RAF was the HC.2, a high-performance development of the HAS.1 with two coupled 1,350-shp Bristol Siddeley Gnome Mk 110/111 shaft turbines. First ordered in August 1961, for transport, ambulance and general purpose duties, it entered service with No 18 Squadron at Odiham in February 1964.

At present the Wessex HC.2 equips No 18 Squadron in Germany and No 72 Squadron and No 240 OCU (Odiham) in Britain and No 28 Squadron in Hong Kong.

With accommodation for up to sixteen troops in addition to its crew of two or three, the HC.2 has a maximum cruising speed of 126 mph. The type also operates as a search and rescue helicopter based at Manston, Valley and Leuchars, and a specially fitted version, the HC.4, equips the Queen's Flight.

Left: a Wessex of No 28 Squadron operating with men of the Royal Hong Kong Police. Below, a pair of Wessex 2s from Singapore.

Hawker Siddeley Dominie

The Hawker Siddeley Dominie T.1 was the first jet-powered navigation trainer specifically designed for the task to enter service with the RAF and first equipped No 1 Air Navigation School at Stradishall in December 1965. In this role the aircraft normally carries one pilot, a supernumery crew (pilot assister), two students and an instructor. The students sit in rearward-facing seats opposite a table and instructional console with a periscopic sextant station behind their seats in the centre fuselage. The Dominie T.1s are now based at No 6 FTS at Finningley and at the RAF College, Cranwell.

Two communications versions of the HS.125 executive jet are in service with No 32 Squadron at Northolt: the CC.1 (equivalent to the Series 400) and the CC.2 (equivalent to the Series 600).

Powered by two 3,310-lb thrust Bristol Siddeley Viper 520 turbojets, the Dominie T.1 has a maximum cruising speed of 472 mph at 25,000 ft for a range of 927 miles.

Short Belfast

The Belfast C.1 was a four-engined transport designed specifically for the carriage of heavy freight, including the largest types of guns, vehicles, guided missiles and miscellaneous loads. It was fitted with 'beaver-tail' rear loading doors capable of accommodating the largest loads. Early aircraft suffered from reduced performance because of suction-drag on the tail and rear fuselage, but after retrospective modification cruising speed was improved from 275 mph to 315 mph, ceiling by 2,000 ft and payload over an average sector by 8,000 lb.

The first aircraft were delivered to No 53 Squadron (the only one to be equipped with the type) in January 1966 but following defence cuts the ten Belfasts built for the RAF were phased out of service and the last had left RAF service by the end of 1976.

BAC Lightning F.6

Known originally as the Mk 3A, this fully-developed production version has a modified wing profile incorporating camber and an outboard leading-edge extension at approximately one-third span which materially reduces subsonic drag and hence improves range. Also included in this version is a substantially enlarged ventral fuel tank of some 600 gal capacity. The prototype first flew in April 1964 and the first squadron to be re-equipped was No 5, which received its aircraft from the end of 1965. Lightning F.6s later equipped No 11, 23, 56, 74 and 111 Squadrons in Fighter (later Strike) Command. From 1974, F-4 Phantoms began a partial replacement of Strike Command Lightning F.6s in the Air Defence role, but Nos 5 and 11 Squadrons of the Binbrook Wing will retain their Lightnings until the 1980s.

Powered by two Rolls-Royce Avon 301 turbojets, rated at 12,690 lb thrust dry or 16,360 lb with re-heat, the Lightning F.6 has an estimated maximum speed of Mach 2.27 (1,500 mph) at 40,000 ft, with a time from brakes-off to 40,000 ft of two-and-a-half minutes. Armament is a pair of Red Top infra-red homing air-to-air missiles and an optional ventral pack with two 30-mm Aden cannon.

Below: Firestreak-equipped Lightning F.6 of No 5 Squadron at RAF Binbrook. Above: this F.6 is fitted with over-wing ferry tanks and two Red Top missiles.

Hawker Siddeley Andover

The Andover C.1 was a rear-loading military transport aircraft which utilised, with minor modifications, the same front fuselage, wing and tail unit as the commercial Hawker Siddeley 748 series 2.

The prototype C.1 first flew in July 1965 and the type first entered service with No 46 Squadron at Abingdon in July 1966 and in December of that year equipped No 52 Squadron of the Far East Air Force based at Seletar, Singapore. In August 1967, Andovers began to replace No 84 Squadron's Beverleys in Aden. By 1968, thirty-one of these tactical transports had been delivered, but the defence cuts of 1975 signalled the withdrawal of the C.1 from service. Six were modified for radio and radar calibration duties and replaced the Argosy E.1s of No 115 Squadron at Brize Norton.

The Andover CC.2 is the RAF's version of the HS.748 Series 2 civil transport and is used for communications duties with No 32 Squadron as well as equipping the Queen's Flight.

BAC VC10

The military version of the VC10 was produced to RAF specification C.239, issued in 1960. Principal differences from the civil version are the use of up-rated Rolls-Royce Conway engines and additional fuel capacity, a side-loading freight door, strengthened floor, rearward facing seats, flight refuelling probe and Artouste auxiliary power unit mounted in the tail cone.

The first RAF aircraft flew in November 1965 and deliveries commenced in July 1966 to No 10 Squadron. By the end of 1967, a total of fourteen VC10s had been delivered, but this figure was cut back after the defence cuts of 1975, and the present strength of No 10 Squadron at Brize Norton is a mere eleven aircraft. The aircraft are all named after winners of the Victoria Cross.

Powered by four 21,000-lb thrust Rolls-Royce Conway R.Co43 turbojets, the VC10 has a maximum speed of 580 mph at 30,000 ft and cruises at 550 mph at 38,000 ft. Standard seating is for 150 passengers and maximum payload is 54,000 lb.

Lockheed Hercules

The RAF acquired sixty-six Hercules C.1s from America to replace Beverleys and Hastings as the standard medium-range tactical transport, the first aircraft arriving in Britain in December 1966. It is equivalent to the USAF's C-130E and is powered by four 4,050-eshp Allison T56-A-7A turboprops, giving it a maximum speed of 384 mph and an economical cruising speed of 340 mph. Maximum range is 4,770 miles.

Following the 1975 defence cuts, thirteen Hercules were withdrawn from front-line service, and the remaining forty-eight aircraft are maintained in Nos 24, 30, 47 and 70 Squadrons at Lyneham, together with an Operational Conversion Unit at the same base. A single Hercules was also converted to W Mk 2 configuration for weather reconnaissance with the Met Research Flight at Farnborough (below).

1969-1978

McDonnell Douglas Phantom

The RAF operates two versions of the American Phantom, generally regarded as one of the best warplanes of the entire post-war period from any nation. The Phantom FG.1 is used in the air defence interceptor role and the FGR.2 is used for ground attack and tactical reconnaissance duties. The first FGR.2s arrived at Aldergrove in July 1968 and the RAF's first operational Phantom squadron, No 6 at Coningsby, formed in May 1969. Subsequently, FGR.2s served with Nos 2, 14, 17, 23, 29, 31, 41, 54, 56 and 111 Squadrons.

As an air defence fighter, the FG.1 first entered service with No 43 Squadron at Leuchars in September 1969. Altogether, 168 Phantoms were delivered to the UK, some of them FG.1s for the Royal Navy. With the introduction of the Sepecat Jaguar into squadron service, the strike Phantoms were gradually changed over to pure air defence duties, replacing some of Strike Command's Lightnings. At present, Phantom FGR.2s serve in the air defence role with Nos 19 and 92 Squadrons in RAF Germany and provide the primary UK air defence force with Nos 29, 111, 23 and 56 Squadrons. These aircraft complement the FG.1s of No 43 Squadron.

Powered by two Rolls-Royce Spey Mk 202 turbofans rated at 12,250 lb thrust dry and 20,515 lb with re-heat, the Phantom is capable of a maximum speed of 1,386 mph at 40,000 ft and has an initial rate of climb of 32,000 ft/min. Armament consists of about 16,000 lb of ordnance for the attack version and four or six AIM-7E Sparrow plus four AIM-9D Sidewinder air-to-air guided missiles for the air defence version.

Centre: accompanied by a Harrier GR.3 from No 3 Squadron, RAF Gütersloh, is an air defence Phantom FGR.2 from No 19 Squadron based at Wildenrath, West Germany, photographed in early 1977. Phantoms are true all-weather aircraft. This FGR.2 (bottom) from No 29 Squadron waits on a rain-soaked dispersal at RAF Coningsby. The Phantom FGR2 of No 6 Squadron in the top photograph is carrying three Sparrow air-to-air missiles and two groups of SNEB rockets. A strike camera (fitted in one of the foward missile bays), fuel tanks and a centre line cannon pod are also shown.

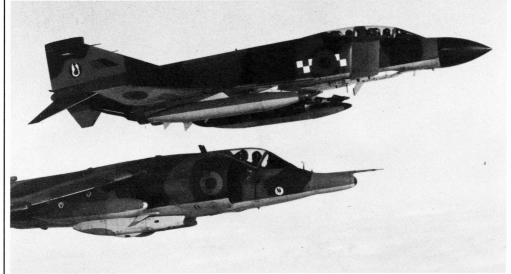

169

Hawker Siddeley Harrier

The Harrier was the world's first operational fixed-wing V/Stol aircraft and was a development of the P.1127 and Kestrel. The first of six development aircraft flew in August 1966 with the first true production aircraft making its maiden flight in December 1967. The single-seat Harrier GR.1 was powered by a 19,000-lb thrust Pegasus 101 engine and first entered service with No 1 Squadron in June 1969. The conversion from Hunter FGA.9s to Harriers was a lengthy process and not

without the problems associated with a revolutionary new aircraft, but by the beginning of 1972 a further three squadrons in RAF Germany, Nos 3, 4 and 20, were successfully operating the Harrier.

The Harrier GR.1A was an updated version of the GR.1 fitted with the 20,000-lb thrust Pegasus 102 engine, and the final production version was the GR.3 with 21,500-lb thrust Pegasus 103 engine and Ferranti Laser Ranging and Marked Target Seeker fitted in an extended nose. The Harrier

GR.3 currently serves with No 1 Squadron and No 233 Operational Conversion Unit at Wittering, and with Nos 3, 4 and 20 Squadrons at Gütersloh, although No 20 Squadron is expected to disband soon. Maximum speed of the GR.3 is 720 mph (Mach 0.95) and cruising speed is 560 mph at 20,000 ft. Tactical radius with two 100-gal drop tanks is 400 miles. Armament includes provision for two 30-mm Aden cannon and up to 5,000 lb of stores on five external hardpoints. Top: these two Harriers from

No 4 Squadron, RAF Germany, do not have the Ferranti laser ranging of the later GR.3s. Demonstrating its independence from the orthodox concrete runways demanded by its more prosaic contemporaries, this Harrier GR.1 (above), also from No 4 Squadron at Wildenrath, rises from the waste ground surrounding the airfield, while secure under camouflage netting, a Harrier GR.3 (left) shows off its new Laser-nose.

BAC Jet Provost Mk 5

The Jet Provost T.5 is a development of the earlier T.4 and includes a fully pressurised cockpit for high altitude training and increased fuel capacity. A total of 110 T.5s was ordered for the RAF, the first of which made its maiden flight at Warton in February 1967. First deliveries were to the Central Flying School at Little Rissington in September 1969 and the aircraft were finished in the new red and white livery standardized for Training Command in June 1968.

Powered by a 2,500-lb thrust Rolls-Royce Viper 201 turbojet, the Jet Provost T.5 has a maximum speed of 440 mph at 25,000 ft and a ceiling of 37,000 ft.

Hawker Siddeley Buccaneer

The Buccaneer was originally designed as a shipboard low-level strike aircraft for the Fleet Air Arm and was chosen for the RAF in 1968 to fill the gap in its strike and photo-reconnaissance capability left by the successive cancellations of the TSR.2, F-111K and AFVG aircraft. Somewhere in the region of one hundred Buccaneers entered service with the RAF, forty-two of which were built from new, the remainder being ex-Fleet Air Arm S.2s.

The first RAF aircraft flew from Brough in January 1969 and the first unit to be equipped with the type was No 12 Squadron at Honington which received the first of its aircraft in October 1969. The second Buccaneer squadron to form was No 15, also at Honington, in October 1970; this squadron moved to RAF Germany in January 1971. Second overseas squadron was No 16 Squadron, which formed in late 1972, and the final home-based Buccaneer

squadron was No 208, which formed at Honington for the overland strike role in July 1974.

Ex-Fleet Air Arm S.2s have been brought up to S.2A standard with avionics and equipment changes, and the S.2B with bomb-bay-door fuel tank and strengthened undercarriage has provision for the Martel missile. Powered by two 11,255-lb thrust Rolls-Royce Spey 101 turbofans, the Buccaneer has a maximum speed of 645 mph at 250 ft and can carry up to 16,000 lb

Above: shown on the outboard pylon of this Buccaneer S.2B is the TV-guided Martel missile. The transmitter/receiver equipment is carried on the white inner pylon. This unusual shot (below) is of two No 208 Squadron aircraft from Honington.

Hawker Siddeley Nimrod

The Nimrod maritime reconnaissance aircraft was developed from the Comet as a Shackleton replacement and first flew in May 1967. The first production Nimrod MR.1 made its maiden flight in June 1968 and the first of forty-six aircraft for the RAF entered service at St Mawgan with No 236 OCU in October 1969. The Nimrod currently equips No 120, 201 and 206 Squadrons at Kinloss, and No 42 Squadron plus the OCU at St Mawgan. No 203 Squadron in Malta was due to disband early in 1978. Eleven of the Mk 1s are being converted to the Airborne

Early Warning role while others are being converted to MR.2 standard. Three Nimrods also operate with No 51 Squadron at Wyton in the Electronic Intelligence (ELINT) role.

Powered by four 12,160-lb thrust Rolls-Royce Spey 250 turbofans, the Nimrod is capable of a maximum speed of 575 mph and has a range of up to 5,755 miles. Armament consists of homing torpedoes and depth charges carried in a ventral bomb-bay plus four AS.12 or Martel air-to-surface missiles carried on wing pylons.

Westland/Aerospatiale Puma

The Puma is a tactical assault and troop transport helicopter carrying a crew of four and up to twenty troops or six stretcher cases plus four seated casualties. First flight of this French-designed helicopter built in Britain was in November 1970, and the first of forty Pumas built for the RAF by Westlands at Hayes was delivered to Air Support Command in January 1971. The type currently equips Nos 33 and 230 Squadrons of No 38 Group Strike Command, based at Odiham.

Powered by two 1,320-shp Turbomeca Turmo IIIC4 engines, the Puma has a top speed of 174 mph at sea level and a maximum range of 390 miles.

Scottish Aviation Bulldog

The Bulldog two-seat primary trainer was a development of the civil Beagle Pup and was taken over by Scottish Aviation originally to honour contracts placed by Sweden, Kenya and Malaysia. A somnambulant Ministry of Defence finally placed a production order for the improved Series 120 aircraft in 1972. The first Bulldog T.1 for the RAF flew in January 1973 and deliveries to the Central Flying School at Little Rissington began in April of that year. Currently the RAF has about 130 Bulldogs equipping the RN Elementary Flying Training Squadron at Leeming, the CFS, also now at Leeming, and sixteen University Air Squadrons, where the Bulldog has replaced the de Havilland Chipmunks.

Powered by a 200-hp Lycoming engine, the Bulldog has a maximum speed of 150 mph at sea level and a cruising speed of 138 mph at 4,000 ft.

Scottish Aviation Jetstream

The Jetstream T.1 multi-engined pilot trainer was originally designed as a civil aircraft by Handley Page. Twenty-six were ordered by the RAF in 1972, the first aircraft making its maiden flight at Prestwick in April 1973. Delivery to the Central Flying School at Little Rissington began in June 1973 and the aircraft began to replace the Varsity at No 5 FTS at Oakington. Most Jetstreams, however, were delivered straight into storage after a decision was taken to suspend multi-engined pilot training because of a pilot surplus. In 1976 the RAF reversed its training policy and eight Jetstreams now equip the Multi-engined Training Squadron at No 3 FTS, Leeming.

Powered by two 940-eshp Turbomeca Astazou XVI turboprops, the Jetstream T.1 has a maximum speed of 285 mph at 12,000 ft and a range of 1,382 miles.

Westland/Aerospatiale Gazelle

The SA 341 Gazelle is produced
jointly by Aerospatiale and Westland Helicopters under an Anglo-
French agreement signed in 1967.
The first prototype, designated SA
340, flew in April 1967 with the first
production SA 341 flying for the
first time in August 1971. The
Gazelle is operated by both the
Army and Royal Navy in addition to
the RAF, which designates its aircraft HT.MK 3. The first of fourteen
HT.3s was delivered to the RAFs
Central Flying School in July 1973,
and the type currently equips No 2
FTS.

Powered by a 590-shp Tur-
bomeca Astazou IIIA turboshaft,
the Gazelle has a maximum cruising speed at sea level of 166 mph
and a range with full fuel of 416
miles.

Handley Page Victor K.2

With the withdrawal of the Victor from bomber and strategic reconnaissance squadrons of the RAF, the type has been undergoing modifications at Hawker Siddeley's Woodford plant to bring it up to K.2 tanker standard. The first deliveries to RAF Marham were in May 1974 and a total of twenty-four currently equips Nos 55 and 57 Squadrons, with training being undertaken by No 232 OCU. Powered by four 20,600-lb thrust Rolls-Royce Conway 201s, the Victor K.2 has a maximum speed of more than 600 mph at above 40,000 ft. Total fuel capacity is 127,000 lb.

Sepecat Jaguar

The Anglo-French Jaguar, which was evolved from the Breguet Br 121 project, was designed by Breguet and BAC to meet a common requirement of the British and French air forces for a dual-role aircraft to be used for advanced and operational training and as a lightweight tactical support aircraft. A naval version for France was abandoned in 1973. The original French-built Jaguar flew in September 1968 and the first BAC-built aircraft flew from Warton in October 1969. The Operational Conversion Unit (No 226) at Lossiemouth received the first of its aircraft in September 1973 and the first RAF Jaguar squadron, No 54, became fully operational at Coltishall in August 1974.

The RAF currently has eight fully operational Jaguar squadrons: Nos 6, 54, and 41 based at Coltishall, with No 41 Squadron operating in the reconnaissance role; Nos 14, 17, 20, and 31 at Brüggen in Germany; and No 2 Squadron at Laarbruch, also in the reconnaissance role. About two hundred Jaguars have been delivered to the RAF to date, of which some 35 are Jaguar T.2 advanced operational trainers.

British Jaguars possess extremely sophisticated nav/attack equipment including the Marconi-Elliott digital/inertial navigation and weapon aiming sub-system known as NAVWASS, as well as a Smiths electronic head-up display and Ferranti laser rangefinder and marked target seeker in a specially modified nose. Armament on the Jaguar GR.1 includes two 30-mm cannon in the lower fuselage aft of the cockpit and up to 10,000 lb of external stores on five hardpoints. Reconnaissance aircraft carry a BAC-designed reconnaissance pod on the fuselage centreline containing optical cameras for horizon-to-horizon coverage and Linescan equipment.

Powered by two Rolls-Royce/Turbomeca Adour Mk 102 turbofans rated at 5,115 lb thrust dry and 7,305 lb thrust with re-heat, maximum speed is estimated to be in the region of Mach 1.1 at 1,000 ft and Mach 1.5 at 36,000 ft.

Superimposed on this photograph of a Jaguar T.2 and GR.1 on final approach is (left) a heavily loaded GR.1 of No 2 Squadron taking off from RAF Laarburch, Germany, while (right) lined up at Coltishall are Jaguars from No 54 Squadron. First and last aircraft in the line are T.1s, while the remainder are GR.1s with laser nose and rearward radar warning aerials in the tail fins.

Westland Sea King HAR.3

The Sea King was originally developed to meet the Royal Navy's requirement for an advanced anti-submarine helicopter. The Sea King programme stemmed from a licence agreement with Sikorsky in America for the S-61, concluded in 1959. The basic airframe is much the same as that for the SH-3D, but considerable differences were made in the power plant and in specialist equipment, to meet British requirements.

In 1975 it was announced that fifteen Sea King HAR.3 helicopters had been ordered to meet an RAF requirement for a long-range search and rescue helicopter, to be based at several sites around the UK, including Coltishall, Boulmer, Brawdy and Lossiemouth. The first aircraft were expected to enter service in the spring of 1978, and will equip Nos 22 and 202 Squadrons.

Powered by two 1,660-shp Rolls-Royce Gnome H.1400-1 turboshafts, the Sea King HAR.3 has a cruising speed of 129mph and a radius of action of about 270 miles, compared with the 85 miles of the Whirlwind and the 95 miles of the Wessex. Accommodation is for up to three stretchers and twelve survivors in addition to the normal crew of four.

Hawker Siddeley Hawk

The Hawk was the winner of an RAF competition for a new advanced jet trainer to replace the Gnat and Hunter T.7 and was selected, as the HS.1182, in October 1971. A production order for 176 Hawks, comprising one pre-production and 175 production aircraft, was placed in March 1972. The first aircraft made its maiden flight in August 1974 and was demonstrated immediately afterwards at the Farnborough Air Show. Since then, six development aircraft have completed the trials programme, including gun firing and spinning clearance and the first two Hawks were handed over to the RAF in November 1976. Currently, six aircraft are with the Central Flying School with a further nineteen at No 4 Flying Training School, both of which are at Valley in Anglesey. Five Hawks also equip the Tactical Weapons Unit at Brawdy, Pembrokeshire.

Powered by a 5,340-lb thrust Rolls-Royce Turbomeca Adour 151 turbofan, the Hawk T.1 is capable of a maximum speed of 647mph in level flight and a maximum Mach No of 1.16. In the weapon training role, the Hawk can carry a 30-mm cannon on the fuselage centreline and a variety of light stores on two underwing hardpoints.

Panavia Tornado

The two-seat Panavia Tornado variable-geometry aircraft, originally known as the MRCA (Multi-Role Combat Aircraft), is currently under development for the armed forces of Britain, West Germany and Italy. The Royal Air Force is expected to order a total of 385 Tornados and these are due to enter service with the OCU at Cottesmore in 1979. In the first instance they will replace the Vulcans and Buccaneers of Nos 9, 12, 15, 16, 35, 44, 50, 101 and 617 Squadrons of Strike Command in the overland strike and reconnaissance roles. Starting in 1983, about 185 air defence Tornados will start replacing Phantoms, and the type is also slated to replace Buccaneers in the maritime strike role. This re-equipment will mean that, ultimately, the Tornado will make up some two-thirds of the RAF's front-line aircraft strength.

The first prototype aircraft made its first flight from Manching in West Germany in August 1974, with the second aircraft flying from BAC's Warton airfield in October of that year. By early 1978, twelve aircraft had flown from the three flight centres in Britain, West Germany and Italy, and of these nine

are prototypes and thrée are pre-production aircraft; a further three pre-production aircraft are scheduled to fly during the course of 1978.

Powered by two Turbo-Union RB 199-43R Mk 101 turbofans rated at 8,500 lb thrust dry and 15,000 lb thrust with re-heat, the Tornado is supposed to have a maximum speed of Mach 1.1 at sea level and Mach 2.2 above 36,000 ft. The nominal maximum weapon load of the attack version is 18,000 lb, carried on three tandem twin pylons under the fuselage, two tandem inboard wing pylons and two single outboard wing pylons. This load, which could include bombs, AS.30, Martel or Kormoran missiles, would incur a heavy fuel penalty. The British air defence variant will embody certain aerodynamic refinements such as semi-recessed missile positions, increased fuel capacity and a longer fuselage. All Tornados will carry two 27-mm Mauser cannon, one in each side of the lower forward fuselage, while the ADV Tornado will have provision for Skyflash and AIM-9L Super Sidewinder air-to-air missiles.

Chronology

1917

29 November: The Air Force (Constitution) Bill given the Royal assent. This provided for the creation of a Royal Air Force and an Air Ministry.

1918

2 January: The Air Ministry established.

1 April: The Royal Air Force established by the amalgamation of the Royal Flying Corps and the Royal Naval Air Service. The first sortie flown by the new Service was despatched on the same day by No 22 Squadron (Bristol Fighters).

14 April: Major-General F. H. Sykes appointed Chief of Air Staff.

May: Decision made to form the Independent Force, RAF.

6 June: The Independent Force, under the command of Major-General Sir Hugh Trenchard, established, comprising Nos 55, 99 and 104 Squadrons.

8 August: The Allies opened the Amiens offensive on the Western Front.

September: The Sopwith Snipe entered service on the Western Front. Eight D.H.4 aircraft arrived at Archangel as the Air Component of the Allied Expeditionary Force in Russia supporting the White faction against that country's revolutionary government.

26 October: Major-General Sir Hugh Trenchard assumed command of Inter-Allied Independent Air Force.

11 November: An Armistice between the Allies and Germany brought an end to the fighting on the Western Front.

29 November: A Handley Page V/1500 flown by Captain Ross Smith made the first flight from Cairo to India, via Baghdad.

1919

11 January: Trenchard re-appointed Chief of Air Staff and Major-General F. H. Sykes appointed Controller-General of Civil Aviation.

12 February: Winston Churchill became Secretary of State for War and Air.

14/15 May: A D.H.10 made the world's first night mail-carrying flight between Hawkinge and Cologne on behalf of the British occupation forces.

June: The treaty of Versailles was signed, formally ending World War One.

July: No 58 Squadron, based in Egypt, received the first Vickers Vimy bomber aircraft. Introduction of Short Service Commissions.

4 August: Present ranks of RAF brought into use.

11 December: Winston Churchill presented a White Paper to Parliament (based on a memorandum drawn up by Trenchard) which outlined the form and duties of the peace-time RAF.

1920

5 February: RAF Cadet College opened at Cranwell.

July: No 55 Squadron despatched to Turkey to reinforce the British forces defending Constantinople and the Dardanelles against Turkish nationalists.

3 July: First RAF Tournament (later known as Pageant and subsequently RAF Display) held at Hendon.

1921

Aircraft from Nos 30, 47 and 70 Squadrons supplied a convoy making a track across the Syrian desert as a navigational aid for the Cairo-Baghdad airmail route.

October: Announced that British Forces in Iraq were to be placed under control of RAF Iraq, which had been part of Middle East Area, subsequently became a separate command and Air Vice-Marshal Sir John Salmond was appointed to command it.

1922

4 April: RAF Staff College opened at Andover.

August: A Metropolitan Air Force, that is, one based in Great Britain, of fourteen bomber and nine fighter squadrons, totalling 266 aircraft, proposed by the Air Staff.

September: Aircraft from No 70 Squadron helped to evacuate the Sulaimaniya garrison in Iraq which was under seige by rebellious tribesmen.

1 October: Military control of Mesopotamia (Iraq) officially taken over by the RAF.

November: No 45 Squadron based at Hinaidi received the first Vickers Vernon transport aircraft.

1923

From Feb to Mar 1923, RAF Cmd. in Iraq executed successful operations against Sheik Mahmud, Governor of Sulaimaniya in S. Kurdistan.

9 February: Formation of the Reserve of Air Force Officers.

2 June: A sub-committee of the Committee for Imperial Defence under the chairmanship of Lord Salisbury met to consider the status of the RAF. It produced proposals to increase the Metropolitan Force to 52 squadrons and advocated the continuance of RAF control over Naval aviation.

October: One flight of No 111 Squadron based at Duxford received the first Gloster Grebe fighter aircraft.

1924

April: Creation of the Fleet Air Arm. No 99 (Bomber) Squadron based at Bircham Newton received the first Avro Aldershots.

May: No 41 Squadron based at Northolt received the first Armstrong Whitworth Siskin III fighter aircraft. In the same month, the official squadron titles incorporated a description of function, i.e., 'bomber', 'fighter', etc.

9 October: Order in Council establishing the Auxiliary Air Force.

Autumn: Nos 7 and 58 (Bomber) Squadrons received the first Vickers Virginia heavy night bomber aircraft.

1925

1 January: The existing Metropolitan squadrons were amalgamated into the Air Defence of Great Britain under the command of Air Marshal Salmond.

February: The RAF undertook operations against the Mahsud tribe in Waziristan. This was the first independent action fought in India by that Service.

May: No 3 (Fighter) Squadron based at Upavon received the first Hawker Woodcock fighter aircraft.

September: No 480 (Coastal Reconnaissance) Flight based at Calshot received the first Supermarine Southampton flying boat. First Auxiliary Air Force Squadron formed. (No 602 (Bomber) Squadron).

22 October: No 1 Apprentices Wing formed at Halton.

25 October: Three aircraft from No 47 (Bomber) Squadron led by Sqn. Ldr. A. Coningham made the first flight from Cairo to Karo, Nigeria. The return flight was completed by 19 November.

1926

1 March: Four Fairey IIID land-planes (S1102, S1103, S1104 and S1105) of the RAF's Cape Flight made the first flight between Heliopolis and Cape Town, arriving at the latter place on 19 April.

April: No 99 (Bomber) Squadron based at Bircham Newton received the first Handley Page Hyderabad heavy night bombing aircraft.

May: No 23 (Fighter) Squadron based at Henlow received the first Gloster Gamecock fighter aircraft.

August	Nos 70 and 216 (Bomber) Squadrons received the first Vickers Victoria transport aircraft. In the same month, No 12 (Bomber) Squadron based at Andover received the first Fairey Fox bomber aircraft.	
September:	No 216 (Bomber) Squadron made a proving flight from Cairo to Aden.	
Autumn:	No 47 (Bomber) Squadron, based at Khartoum, received the first Fairey IIIF general purpose aircraft.	

1927 Nos 2 and 100 (Bomber) Squadrons received the first Hawker Horsley bomber aircraft.

May: A modified Horsley (J8607) flown by F/Lt. Carr and F/Lt. Gillman attempted a non-stop flight from Cranwell to India. The aircraft was forced down in the Persian Gulf after flying 3,420 miles in 4.5 hours. This was an unofficial long distance record which was shortly overtaken by Lindberg's New York-Paris flight.

Summer: The Armstrong Whitworth Siskin IIIA entered service with Nos 1 and 56 (Fighter) Squadrons.

25 July: The Air Defence of Great Britain force held its first annual exercise.

26 September: The Supermarine S.5 N220 flown by F/Lt. Webster won the Schneider Trophy for Great Britain at an average speed of 273.07 mph. During the same contest, Webster established a new World Speed Record over 100 km of 283.6 mph.

October: No 26 (Army Co-operation Squadron) received the first Armstrong Whitworth Atlas aircraft.

17 October: Far East Flight, led by Group Captain Cave-Brown-Cave, left England for Singapore in four Supermarine Southampton flying boats.

1928

February: Defence of Aden placed under RAF control.

March: No 101 (Bomber) Squadron based at Bircham Newton received the first Boulton Paul Sidestrand bomber aircraft.

23 December: Aircraft from Nos 27 and 70 (Bomber) Squadrons began to evacuate personnel from Kabul in Afghanistan which was being threatened by the forces of Habidullah Khan.

1929

May: No 3 (Fighter) Squadron based at Upavon received the first Bristol Bulldog Fighter aircraft.

6/7 September: Supermarine S.6 N247 flown by F/O. Waghorn won the Schneider Trophy for Great Britain at an average speed of 328.63 mph. During the same contest, another S.6 N248 flown by F/O. Atcherley established new World Speed Records over 60 and 100 km of 332 and 331 mph respectively.

12 September: Supermarine S.6 N247 flown by Sq/Ldr. Orlebar set up a new World Absolute Speed Record of 357.7 mph.

1930

30 April: No 33(B) Squadron based at Eastchurch received the first Hawker Hart light bomber.

2 July: An RAF Blackburn Iris III flying boat made the first non-stop flight from Iceland to the UK.

November: No 26(B) Squadron became the first land-based torpedo bomber unit of the RAF to be stationed overseas (at Singapore).

1931 The Short Rangoon flying boat entered service with No 203 Squadron based at Basrah. During the year, No 6 Squadron became involved in the Arab-Jewish conflict in Palestine.

January: No 216 Squadron flew the first route proving flight between Egypt and Cape Town.

April: No 40 Squadron based at Upper Heyford received the first Fairey Gordon light bomber.

May: The Hawker Demon two-seat fighter entered service with one flight of No 23 Squadron.

June: The Hawker Fury entered service with No 43 Squadron at Tangmere.

September: The first Instrument Flying course opened at the CFS at Wittering.

12 September: The Supermarine S.6B S1595, flown by F/Lt. Bootham won the Schneider Trophy for all time for Great Britain at an average speed of 340.08 mph.

29 September: The Supermarine S.6B, S1596, flown by F/Lt. Stainforth set up an absolute World Speed Record of 407.5 mph. S1596 was the first aircraft to exceed 400 mph in level flight.

Autumn: The de Havilland Tiger Moth trainer entered service with the RAF.

1932 British troops were airlifted from Egypt to Cyprus by Vickers Victorias of No 216 Squadron.

February: The Hawker Audax light bomber entered service with No 4 Squadron based at Farnborough.

March: No 216 Squadron made the first route proving flight between Egypt and Somaliland.

1933 The Vickers Vildebeest torpedo bomber entered service with No 100 Squadron at Donibristle.

Spring: The Westland Wallace light bomber entered service with No 501 Squadron.

February: The Fairey Long-range Monoplane, flown by Sqn/Ldr. O. R. Gayford and F/Lt. G. E. Nicholetts, captured the world's long distance record with a flight of 5,309 miles between Cranwell and Walvis Bay, SW Africa, (flight time 57 hours 25 minutes).

August: The Saro Cloud flying boat entered service with B Flight of the Seaplane Training Squadron at Calshot.

November: The Handley Page Heyford heavy bomber entered service with No 99 Squadron at Upper Heyford. The Heyford was the RAF's last heavy bomber biplane.

1934 The Blackburn Perth Flying Boat entered service with No 209 Squadron at Mount Batten. In the same year, No 101 Squadron was equipped with the Boulton Paul Overstrand medium bomber.

24 May: First Empire Air Day held with RAF stations opening to the public.

July: Baldwin's government announced its intention to increase the RAF's front line strength by 41 squadrons over a five-year period.

Autumn: The Vickers Vincent entered service with No 8 Squadron at Aden.

December: The School of Army Co-operation at Old Sarum began trials with the Avro Rota autogyro.

1935 The Hawker Hardy light bomber entered service with No 30 Squadron at Mosul.

March: Re-establishment of the *Luftwaffe* (German Air Force) was made public.

April: The Short Singapore III flying boat entered service with No 230 Squadron at Pembroke Dock.

May: The Gloster Gauntlet fighter entered service with No 19 Squadron at Duxford.

22 May: Proposals laid before Parliament to raise first-line aircraft strength to 1,500 by 1937.

6 July: King George V reviewed RAF at Mildenhall and Duxford.

3 October: Italy declared war on Abyssinia. The RAF in the Middle East was strengthened and put on the alert.

Autumn: The Hawker Hind light bomber entered service with Nos 18, 21 and 34 Squadrons, all based at Bircham Newton.

1936 The Supermarine Stranraer flying boat entered service with No 228 Squadron at Pembroke Dock.

February: The Khartoum-West Africa civil air route opened after survey work carried out by No 216 Squadron.

March: The Avro Anson general reconnaissance/light bomber aircraft entered service with No 48 Squadron at Manston.

14 July:	Metropolitan Air Force re-organised into Fighter, Bomber, Coastal and Training Commands.
30 July:	Formation of Royal Air Force Volunteer Reserve.
September:	The Bristol 138A flown by S/Ldr. Swain reached an altitude of 48,698 ft and captured the World Altitude Record for Great Britain.
November:	The Fairey Hendon entered service with No 38 Squadron at Mildenhall. The Hendon was the RAF's first all-metal low wing cantilever monoplane.

1937

January:	The Bristol Blenheim bomber entered service with No 114 Squadron at Wyton. During the same month, Nos 3 and 72 Squadrons received the first Gloster Gladiator fighters.
February:	The Hawker Hector light bomber entered service with No 4 Squadron at Odiham.
March:	The Fairey Battle light bomber entered service with No 63 Squadron at Upwood. During the same month, the Armstrong Whitworth Whitley heavy bomber entered service with No 10 Squadron at Dishforth.
April:	The Handley Page Harrow heavy bomber entered service with No 214 Squadron at Feltwell. During the same month, the Vickers Wellesley long-range bomber entered service with No 76 Squadron at Finningley.
May:	The first Chain Home radar station in the UK early warning chain was taken into RAF service.
June:	The Bristol 138A flown by F/Lt. Adam reached an altitude of 53,937 ft and regained the World Altitude Record from Italy.
Mid-year:	The Hawker Fury II entered service with No 25 Squadron at Hawkinge.
30 July:	The Admiralty took over complete control of the Fleet Air Arm.
November:	The Airspeed Oxford trainer entered service with the CFS.
December:	The Hawker Hurricane entered service with No 111 Squadron at Northolt.

1938

February:	S/Ldr. Gilian of No 111 Squadron flew a Hurricane from Edinburgh to Northolt in 48 minutes, an average speed of 408 mph.
June:	The Supermarine Spitfire entered service with No 19 Squadron at Duxford.
Summer:	The Short Sunderland flying boat entered service with No 210 Squadron at Pembroke Dock.
August:	The Handley Page Hampden bomber entered service with No 49 Squadron.
September:	The Munich crisis caused the RAF to be placed on a war footing.
October:	The Vickers Wellington bomber entered service with No 99 Squadron at Mildenhall.
November:	Three Wellesleys (L2638, L2639 and L2680) made the attempt to fly non-stop from Egypt to Australia. L2638 and L2680 completed the journey, landing at Darwin on the 7th of the month after a flight of just over 48 hours and 7,162 miles. This flight set up a new World Long-Distance Record.
Late 1938:	The Westland Lysander army co-operation aircraft entered service with No 16 Squadron at Old Sarum.

1939

Spring:	The Bristol Bombay bomber-transport entered service with No 117 Squadron.
Summer:	The Lockheed Hudson general reconnaissance aircraft entered service with No 224 Squadron at Gosport.
23 August:	RAF units partially mobilised to war establishment.
1 September:	Germany invaded Poland.
3 September:	Britain, Australia, New Zealand and France declared war on Germany.
4 September:	First RAF bombing raid of the war when Blenheims of Nos 107 and 110 Squadrons and Wellingtons of Nos 9

	and 149 Squadrons attacked German warships near Wilhelmshaven and Brunsbuttel.
20 September:	The first enemy aircraft was destroyed by the RAF when the rear gunner of a No 88 Squadron Battle shot down a Bf 109 over France.
October:	The Blackburn Botha general reconnaissance aircraft entered service with No 608 Squadron at Thornaby.
16 October:	The first German raid on Britain was made against the Firth of Forth area. Two enemy aircraft were claimed by RAF fighters.
December:	The Bristol Beaufort torpedo bomber entered service with No 22 Squadron at Thorney Island.
17 December:	The Empire Air Training Scheme began.
18 December:	Twenty-four Wellingtons of Nos 9, 37 and 149 Squadrons lost at least 12 of their number during a raid against the Wilhelmshaven area. This attack marked the end of RAF attempts to bomb German targets in daylight until 1944.

1940

11 March:	The RAF sank its first U-boat when a Blenheim of No 82 Squadron bombed U-31 in the Schillig Roads.
25 April:	Gladiators of No 263 Squadron began operations from Norway. By the 28th, the Squadron had been destroyed.
10 May:	German forces began the invasion of Holland, Belgium and Luxembourg. Churchill became Prime Minister.
22 May:	No 263 Squadron, along with No 46 (Hurricane) Squadron, returned to Norway, defending Narvik until the end of the campaign.
26 May:	The evacuation of British forces in France began at Dunkirk, ending on 4 June.
11 June:	Whitleys of Nos 10, 51, 77 and 102 Squadrons made the first bombing raid on the Italian mainland (Turin).
18 June:	The last RAF unit was evacuated from France. Operations in the Low Countries and France had cost the RAF 959 aircraft including 432 Hurricane and Spitfire fighters.
10 July:	The opening phase of the Battle of Britain began with the Luftwaffe attacking Channel convoys.
15 July:	Bomber Command began its attack on the barges being concentrated for an invasion of Britain.
Summer:	The Westland Whirlwind fighter entered service with No 263 Squadron at Drem.
August:	The Short Stirling heavy bomber entered service with No 7 Squadron at Leeming. The Stirling was the RAF's first four-engined heavy bomber.
8 August:	Second phase of the Battle of Britain began with heavy attacks on convoys, coastal towns and fighter airfields.
25 August:	The first RAF attack on Berlin.
Late August:	Third phase of the Battle of Britain with the Luftwaffe concentrating its bombing raids on London.
September:	The Bristol Beaufighter heavy fighter entered service with No 25 Squadron. During the same month, the Bell Airacobra fighter entered service with No 601 Squadron. The Airacobra was the RAF's first operational aircraft filled with a tricycle undercarriage.
October:	The Martin Maryland reconnaissance bomber entered service with No 431 Flight at Malta.
31 October:	The daylight Battle of Britain ended. Night attacks on London and the towns of the Midlands, which began on 7 September, continued on into the new year (the 'Blitz').
November:	The Avro Manchester heavy bomber entered service with No 207 Squadron at Waddington. During the same month, the Handley Page Halifax heavy bomber entered service with No 35 Squadron at Leeming.
December:	The Douglas Havoc fighter/intruder entered service with No 85 Squadron at West Malling.
16 December:	The first Bomber Command 'area' attack on a German target (Mannheim).

1941

10 January:	The first RAF 'Circus' operation. Circuses were offensive sweeps designed to draw the *Luftwaffe* into battle over occupied Europe.
6 April:	German forces invade Greece and Yugoslavia. RAF aircraft fought in this area until 2 May when the last Imperial forces were evacuated from Greece. During the campaign, the RAF lost 198 aircraft and claimed 350 Italian and German aircraft destroyed.
May:	The Boeing Fortress I heavy bomber entered service with No 90 Squadron at West Raynham.
2 May:	RAF station at Habbaniya in Iraq attacked by German backed rebel forces. No 4 Training School became operational and beat off the attack.
15 May:	The Gloster Whittle E.28/39, the RAF's first jet aircraft, made its first flight from Cranwell.
20 May:	Crete was invaded in a large scale German airborne operation. The available RAF aircraft were quickly overwhelmed and the island was evacuated by the 31st.
Spring:	The Consolidated Catalina Flying Boat entered service with No 209 Squadron at Castle Archdale.
June:	The Consolidated Liberator heavy bomber entered service with No 120 Squadron at Nutts Corner.
22 June:	The Germans invaded the Soviet Union.
July:	The Taylorcraft Auster AOP aircraft entered service with No 651 Squadron.
August:	The Curtiss Tomohawk fighter entered service with No 2 Squadron. During the same month, Nos 81 and 134 Squadrons began operations from Vaenga in Northern Russia with Hurricanes.
11 August:	The first RAF use of the *Gee* navigational aid.
September:	The Hawker Typhoon fighter bomber entered service with No 56 Squadron at Duxford.
Autumn:	The de Havilland Mosquito IV bomber entered service with No 105 Squadron at Marham.
December:	The Avro Lancaster heavy bomber entered service with No 44 Squadron at Waddington.
8 December:	Britain and USA declared war on Japan after the attack on Pearl Harbour.
Winter:	The Douglas Boston intruder/bomber aircraft entered service with No 88 Squadron at Swanton Morley.

1942

January:	The Curtiss Mohawk fighter entered service with No 5 Squadron in India.
5 February:	British forces surrendered to the Japanese in Singapore.
March:	The Martin Baltimore light bomber entered service with No 223 Squadron in North Africa.
April:	The North American Mustang I entered service with No 2 Squadron at Sawbridgeworth.
May:	The de Havilland Mosquito II night fighter entered service with No 23 Squadron at Ford.
30 May:	The first '1,000 bomber' raid, against Cologne.
June:	The Douglas Dakota transport aircraft entered service with No 31 Squadron in Burma.
July:	The first night sinking of a U-boat by an RAF Wellington equipped with a 'Leigh Light' airborne searchlight. In the same month, the Martin Marauder medium bomber entered service with No 14 Squadron in the Middle East.
1 July:	The Axid advance in North Africa was halted at El Alamein.
August:	The Boeing Fortress II reconnaissance bomber entered service with No 59 Squadron at Thorney Island.
15 August:	The Pathfinder Force was formed within Bomber Command.
October:	The Lockheed Venture bomber entered service with No 21 Squadron. In the same month, the North American Mitchell medium bomber entered service with No 98 Squadron.

1943

January:	The Armstrong Whitworth Albermarle glider tug/transport aircraft entered service with No 295 Squadron.
March:	Bomber Command's 'Battle of the Ruhr' began.
1 April:	Twenty-fifth anniversary of the foundation of the RAF.
16 May:	The Mohne and Eder Dams were breached by No 617 Squadron.
1 June:	The formation of the Second Tactical Air Force for the coming invasion of Europe.
Summer:	The Vickers Warwick reconnaissance bomber entered service with No 280 Squadron at Langham.
9 July:	Operation Husky, the invasion of Sicily. This marked the first major Allied airborne operation.
24 July:	First 'fire storm' created in a German target, Hamburg. This date also marked the first use of the *Window* electronic counter-measure which crippled Germany's night defences.
August:	The Sikorsky Hoverfly helicopter entered service with No 529 Squadron. The Hoverfly was the first helicopter to enter service with the RAF.
1 September:	Allied forces invaded Southern Italy.
8 November:	100(SD) Group formed within Bomber Command to operate electronic counter-measures in support of the bomber offensive.
18 November:	Bomber Command began the 'Battle of Berlin'.
Winter:	The Supermarine Sea Otter entered service with the RAF. In the same month, the Martin Mariner flying boat entered service with No 524 Squadron at Oban.

1944

February:	The North American Mustang III fighter entered service with No 19 Squadron at Ford.
30 March:	Bomber Command's greatest loss (95) on a single mission for the entire war (Nuremberg).
April:	The Hawker Tempest V fighter entered service with No 3 Squadron at Newchurch.
5 June:	The Allied invasion of France (Operation Overlord).
7 June:	The RAF Balkan Air Force was formed.
12 June:	The first V-1 pilotless missile was launched against the UK.
July:	The Gloster Meteor jet fighter entered service with No 616 Squadron at Culmhead. The Meteor was the RAF's first jet fighter to become operational.
7 October:	The first use of the 'Tallboy' 12,000 lb bomb.
16 December:	The German Ardennes offensive began.

1945

14 March:	The first use of the 'Grand Slam' 22,000 lb bomb.
8 May:	German Forces in the West surrendered to the Allies.
15 July:	The British Air Forces of Occupation formed in Germany.
6 August:	First atomic bomb dropped on Hiroshima.
14 August:	Japan surrendered to the Allies.
Autumn:	The Avro Lincoln heavy bomber entered service with No 57 Squadron at East Kirby.
7 November:	Gloster Meteor F.4 flown by Group Captain H. J. Wilson raised the world absolute speed limit to 606.4 mph at Herne Bay.

1946

Spring:	The de Havilland Hornet fighter entered service with No 64 Squadron at Horsham St Faith. During the same period, the de Havilland Vampire jet fighter entered service with No 247 Squadron. RAF units were operational against Indonesian nationalists.
2 June:	The Auxiliary Air Force was re-formed with 13 day-fighter, 3 night-fighter and 4 light bomber squadrons.
7 September:	Gloster Meteor F.4 flown by Group Captain E. M. Donaldson raised the world air speed record to 615.8 mph at Littlehampton.

1947
16 December: The AAF became the Royal Auxiliary Air Force.

1948
June: Operations against Communist insurgents in Malaya began (Operation *Firedog*).
28 June: The RAF began to participate in the Berlin airlift (Operation *Plainfare*).
July Six Vampires of No 54 Squadron made the first crossing of the Atlantic by RAF jet aircraft.
October: The Handley Page Hastings transport entered service with No 47 Squadron at Dishforth.

1949
February: Women's Auxiliary Air Force re-named Women's Royal Air Force.
Spring: The Bristol Brigand light bomber entered service with No 84 Squadron at Habbaniyah.
11 May: The Communist blockade of Berlin which had precipitated Operation *Plainfare* was lifted.
1 June: Far East Air Force formed, commanded by Air Marshal Sir Hugh Lloyd.

1950
Spring: The de Havilland Chipmunk trainer entered service with the Oxford University Air Squadron.
March: The Boeing Washington heavy bomber entered service with No 149 Squadron at Marham.
25 June: North Korean forces crossed the 38th parallel and invaded South Korea.

1951
The Armstrong Whitworth Meteor NF.11 entered service with No 29 Squadron at Tangmore. This Mark of the Meteor was the RAF's first jet night fighter.
Spring: The Vampire NF.10 night fighter entered service with No 25 Squadron at West Malling.
February: The Avro Shackleton maritime reconnaissance aircraft entered service with an Operational Conversation Unit at Kinloss.
May: The English Electric Canberra bomber entered service with No 101 Squadron at Binbrook. The Canberra was the RAF's first jet bomber.
September: The British Air Forces of Occupation in Germany became the Second Tactical Air Force.

1952
Spring: The de Havilland Venom fighter bomber entered service with No 11 Squadron in Germany.
April: The Lockheed Neptune anti-submarine aircraft entered service with No 217 Squadron at Kinloss.
3 October: The first British Atomic bomb was exploded in the Monte Bello Islands.

1953
The de Havilland Venom NF.2 night fighter entered service with No 23 Squadron at Cottishall. During the year a new flying training system was introduced in which basic training was carried out on the Provost with advanced flying training on the Vampire T.11.
April: The Bristol Sycamore helicopter entered service with No 275 Squadron at Linton-on-Ouse.
15 July: The RAF Coronation Review by H.M. the Queen.
December: The North American Sabre fighter entered service with No 66 Squadron at Linton-on-Ouse. The Sabre was the RAF's first swept-wing jet fighter.

1954
The Westland Whirlwind helicopter entered service with No 155 Squadron in the Far East.
February: The Supermarine Swift fighter entered service with No 56 Squadron.
November: The Hunting Percival Provost trainer entered service with the RAF College Cranwell.

1955
February: The Vickers Valiant heavy bomber entered service with No 138 Squadron at Gaydon. The Valiant was the first of the RAF's 'V-bombers'.
April: The Hawker Hunter fighter entered service with No 98 Squadron in Germany.
August: The Hunting Percival Jet Provost entered service with No 2 Flying Training School at Hullavington.

1956
February: The Gloster Javelin all-weather fighter entered service with No 46 Squadron at Odinham.
March: The Blackburn Beverley transport entered service with No 47 Squadron at Abingdon.
July: The de Havilland Comet transport entered service with No 216 Squadron at Lyneham. The Comet was the RAF's first jet transport aircraft.
31 October: British and French aircraft attacked targets in Egypt during the 'Suez Crisis'.

1957
April: The Government's Defence White Paper brought about the cancellation of various projects which were to severely affect the RAF's operational capability in the following decade.
May: The Avro Vulcan heavy bomber entered service with No 83 Squadron at Waddington.
15 May: Britain's first hydrogen bomb was dropped at Christmas Island by a Valiant of No 49 Squadron.

1958
13 February: Defence White Paper stated that British megaton bombs were now in production and deliveries to RAF had begun.
April: The Handley Page Victor heavy bomber entered service with No 10 Squadron at Cottesmore.
August: The first RAF unit to be equipped with the Thor intercontinental ballistic missile became operational.

1959
February: Memorandum accompanying 1959-60 Air Estimates stated that a contract was being let for the development of the TSR-2.
18 April: First live firing of Thor by an RAF crew at Vandenberg AFB, California, by launch crew from No 98 Squadron, Driffield.

1960
March: Deployment of Bomber Command's Thor IRBM's completed.
13 April: Minister of Defence (Mr. Harold Watkinson) announced that the Government was abandoning development of Blue Streak missile as a military weapon because of increasing vulnerability to attack of fixed-site missiles.
July: The English Electric Lightning entered service with No 74 Squadron.
31 July: End of emergency campaign against terrorists in Malaya (Operation *Firedog*).
7 October: Minister of Defence (Mr. Harold Watkinson) announced the placing of full development contract for TSR-2.

1961
February: Middle East Air Force re-named Near East Air Force (H.Q. Cyprus); British Forces Arabian Peninsula re-named Air Forces Middle East (H.Q. Aden).
20 July: First non-stop flight UK to Australia by Vulcan 1A of No 617 Squadron; 11,500 miles in 20hr 3min, 573 mph, (refuelled in air three times by Valiant tankers operating from Cyprus, Pakistan and Singapore).
1 July: Following request from ruler of Kuwait for British assistance, RAF Hunter ground-attack fighters and transport aircraft with troops, sent to Kuwait. Canberra squadrons concentrated in Persian Gulf area and V-bombers at readiness in Malta.

1962

June:	RAF celebrated the 50th Anniversary of military aviation in Britain with a flying display at Upavon.
October:	Cuba Crisis; Bomber Command nuclear force alerted.
December:	Skybolt cancelled. Confrontation with Indonesia.

1963

May:	V-bomber force assigned to NATO and integrated into SACEUR.
Summer:	Transport Command Britannias airlifted troops to British Guiana.

1964

January:	Ballistic Missile Early Warning Unit at RAF Fylingdales became fully operational.
February:	Secretary of State for Air disclosed that the V-force was now equipped and trained to attack targets from low level. Aircraft and the Blue Steel stand-off bomb had been modified to operate at no greater height than was necessary to keep safely clear of the ground.
1 April:	Air Ministry became the Air Force department of the Ministry of Defence, the Air Council became the Air Force Board, and the Secretary of State for Air became Minister of Defence for the RAF.
October:	Tripartite Kestrel (P.1127) Squadron formed at RAF West Raynham.

1965

February:	Hawker P.1154 cancelled.
April:	BAC TS2.2 cancelled.
May:	Victor aircraft took over the in-flight refuelling task for the RAF in place of the grounded Valiants, when No 55 Squadron at Marham received its first tanker aircraft.

1966

February:	RAF ordered 50 General Dynamics F.111K swing-wing bombers from USA.

1967

February:	The Defence White Paper announced the merger of Bomber and Fighter Commands, to take place in April, 1968.

1968

January:	Massive Defence cuts were announced with a run-down of RAF personnel, withdrawal from the Far East and Persian Gulf and the cancellation of the fifty General Dynamics F-111K bombers ordered in February 1966.
30 April:	Bomber and Fighter Command merged to form Strike Command.
June:	The Hawker Siddeley Harrier entered service with No 1 Squadron at Wittering.
December:	Handley Page Victor B.2 withdrawn from operationa use with the disbanding of the Wittering Wing (Nos 100 and 139 Squadrons).

1969

March:	Akrotiri Strike Wing of Canberras (Nos 6, 32, 73, 249 Squadrons) disbanded.
May:	The McDonnell Douglas Phantom strike aircraft entered service with No 69 Squadron at Coningsby.
July:	The nuclear deterrent role of Strike Command was relinquished to the Royal Navy's Polaris submarines and the first of the RAF's Blue Steel-equipped Vulcan squadrons disbanded.
October:	Strike Command's first Buccaneer unit No 12 Squadron, re-formed at Honington as the first of four planned squadrons at Honington.

1972

June:	Last operational Canberra bomber squadron disbanded. It was No 16 Squadron at Laarbruch in Germany with Canberra B(1).8s.
August:	Contract signed for the development of the Multi-Role Combat Aircraft.
October:	RAF Germany's Buccaneer Wing complete with re-forming of No 16 Squadron at Laarbruch.

1973

November:	Vulcan entered service in the Strategic Reconnaissance role with No 27 Squadron.

1974

March:	The Sepecat Jaguar strike aircraft entered service with No 54 Squadron at Losslemouth.
14 August:	First flight of the prototype MRCA at Manching.
December:	Defence Minister announces further cuts in RAF establishments.

1978

1 April:	The 60th Anniversary of the RAF. On 1 April 1918, the RAF had a front line strength of some 2,500 aircraft; sixty years later that number is 400 . . .

Index

191